HOW TO LIVE
JAPANESE

WHITE LION
PUBLISHING

Introduction

Tokyo is an overwhelming place, even for the Japanese. The city itself – officially known as Tokyo Metropolis – contains over 13 million people. The commuter region immediately around it is home to almost 44 million. In the era of megacities, Tokyo is the biggest of all.

When I come home to Tokyo from overseas, what always strikes me, is that nearly all the people are Japanese. It may sound obvious, but the level of diversity one gets accustomed to in other major cities of the world – ethnically, culturally, aesthetically – is comparatively absent in Tokyo. At least at first glance. Chinese cities may come close in such racial homogeneity, but in Tokyo, the visual uniformity swallows you up, especially during the busy commuting hours. There is a sense of claustrophobia on a grand scale. And that is the first paradox you encounter in Japan. What appears to be the same can be very different in millions of not so obvious ways. Here, diversity is deep, if subtle.

Tokyo is a relatively young city. It was established in 1603 in the village of Edo as the capital city of the Tokugawa shogunate – a new military government – while Japan's emperor remained in the formal capital of Kyoto. Edo flourished, with major civil engineering improvements such as vast land reclamation, the redirecting of major rivers, and aqueducts serving the growing population. However, Edo, and later Tokyo, also suffered several fires, earthquakes, more fires, more earthquakes and, most recently, American carpet bombing during the Second World War.

When the shogunate finally fell, the Emperor went to stay at the now-empty Edo Castle as a temporary measure. Kyoto, the main capital since 794, is still waiting for the return of their Emperor.

Tokyo is essentially the world's foremost scrap-and-build-city. Tokyo Tower, the city's most iconic postwar building, was built with the scrap metal from Sherman tanks used in the Korean war which the Americans didn't bother to ship back home. There is another paradox there. In Japan, what appears old is new, and vice versa.

Of course, Tokyo is only one part of Japan. Over 70 per cent of the country is mountainous, and two-thirds is covered by forest. Nature also makes its presence known through periodic typhoons and more-frequent-than-good-for-peace-of-mind earthquakes. The world-famous Shinkansen bullet train shoots across the front of Mount Fuji, one of the many volcanoes which are actively dormant (or dormant-ly active, depending on which geologist you listen to). Despite having some of the world's most advanced technology, for the Japanese, their environment instils both fear and reverence. European-style religious ferment didn't take hold in Japan, but the Shinto belief in animism still exists in its ancient, raw elements. You can see examples of this in animated films created by the likes of Hayao Miyazaki's Studio Ghibli.

What follows in this book is my personal attempt to explain these paradoxes, topic by topic, so that you may gain some depth to the images of Japan that meet your eyes – to give you a sense of Japan in '3-D', as it were.

日
本
の
生
き
方

4

As a personal attempt, I freely admit that my expositions are not free from subjective prejudice, borne out of my upbringing and experiences. For the sake of fairness, I will make them clear at the outset. I was born in 1970 on the outskirts of Tokyo, and brought up there until I was 19 years old. As a result, I am naturally partial to Tokyo's ways, as opposed to living in the country or even life in provincial cities. You would be correct to sense elements of a superiority complex in my way of describing the provinces, cities and towns outside Tokyo. It creeps in against my better judgment. I have spent most of my adult life living abroad. I was in the UK for 11 years, there were nine years in Hong Kong, and a year in New York, before returning to Japan at the age of 42. I would like to think, therefore, that I share at least some of the perspectives of non-Japanese people in looking at my own country.

You might also feel that I am overcritical in relation to some aspects of Japanese society. I have two answers to that. Firstly, make no mistake: I love my country. However, as Malcolm X said, you are not supposed to be so blind with patriotism that you cannot face reality. There is something wrong if your moral compass takes second place to loving your country. I have tried to be honest to my own values and sensibilities in writing this. In that sense, this is truly personal.

Secondly, I believe that modern Japanese people are, by nature, self-critical. As a result, they are also, in general, insecure. This is historical in its origin. Our country, closed to foreigners, had been ruled by the samurai, who were supposed to be superhumanly brave and strong. But they did not stand a chance against the 'Black Ships' – the Europeans, and later on, Americans – who forced Japan open. The old order collapsed.

The American ships arrived in the 19th century, which is almost just yesterday in terms of our long history. Ever since, in the shadow of western imperialism, we asked ourselves if we had become 'good enough' to stand on our own. That question acquired a renewed sense of urgency following two atomic bombs and defeat in the Second World War. More recently, the rise of nearby China has added relevance to that question. We are a nation obsessed with a sense of obligation to improve ourselves, and insecurity runs deep to the core of our character.

You may find other traits of my partiality of which I am not as aware as those mentioned above. I thank you in advance for your kind generosity in accepting them as my personal shortcomings, and hope that you find what follows nevertheless informative.

Areas of Japan

Okinawa region
沖縄地方

Chūgoku · Shikoku
regions
中国・四国地方

Ho
re
北

KYOTO

Kyushu
region
九州地方

OSA

近畿地方
Kinki region

Hokkaido region
北海道

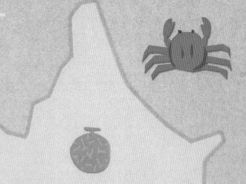

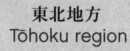

Kōshin'etsu region
甲信越地方

東北地方
Tōhoku region

TOKYO
●東京

関東地方
Kantō region

地方
egion

Kantō 関東地方

Kantō is the area around Tokyo (東京), made up of seven prefectures: Tokyo, Kanagawa, Chiba, Saitama, Gunma, Tochigi and Ibaraki. From the old capital of Kyoto, it was the eastern frontier land, with the name 'Kantō' meaning 'east of the toll gate'. It was also sometimes called 'Bandō', meaning 'east of the slope', as travellers from Kyoto saw the huge marshy plain emerging in front of them as they descended from the central mountainous region.

The samurai thrived in Kantō. When the first shogunate government was established in the 12th century, it chose the city of Kamakura, in present-day Kanagawa prefecture, as its capital. Thus started an age-long rivalry between east and west in Japan. In response to Kantō or Bandō, people gave the name 'Kansai' (関西地方) to the area around Kyoto (and later Osaka), meaning 'west of the toll gate'. To this day, the difference in culture and dialects between the two areas are often highlighted, rather than ignored. Kantō people generally regard Kansai as old-fashioned, while Kansai people think those from Kantō are unsophisticated and dour. Even in the highly homogenised Japanese society of today, Kansai people tend to stick to their native accents when speaking among themselves.

I am Kantō-born, and spent little time outside the region until adulthood. I married a woman from Kansai, and must admit that I panicked a little when I first heard her speaking with her friends from Kansai in their native accents.

The differences extend to foods. Sushi, tempura and soba noodles originated from Edo, and are regarded as Kantō foods. Kansai people say that Kantō foods are too salty, while Kantō people complain that Kansai foods are bland. Still, the culinary rivalry is more friendly than in sport. In baseball, the rivalry between Tokyo's Yomiuri Giants and Kansai's Hanshin Tigers, continues to be fierce.

日
本
の
生
き
方

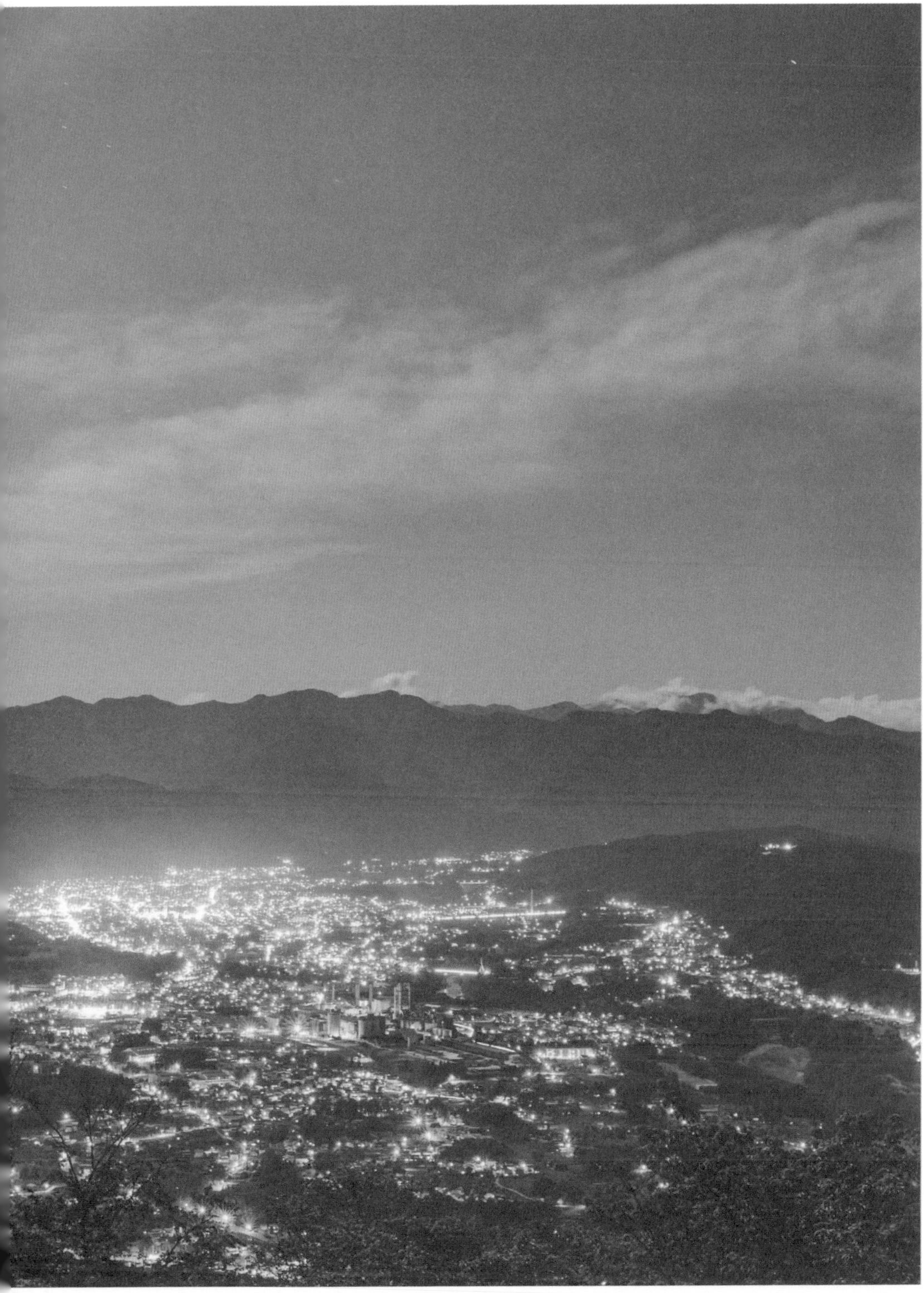

Kyoto 京都

When a city has been the capital for a millennium, even with inevitable ups and downs along the way, it cannot help but grow a character. Kyoto is definitely a character.

Kyoto, or Heian-kyō as it was called at the time, was established as a capital city in 794 by Emperor Kanmu, who wanted to break free from the established courtiers and religious powers based around the ancient capital of Nara (奈良). The deciding factor for the choice of real estate was the Chinese art of feng shui, which advised that a city must have mountains to the north, a river to the east, a lake to the south and major roads to the west. In reality, the main factor was the abundant supply of fresh water provided by the mountains surrounding Kyoto to the north, east and west. One of Kyoto's major tourist attractions to this day is the majestic Kiyomizu-dera (清水寺), a temple perched on the cliff to the east of the city. Kiyomizu literally means 'fresh water'.

As the seat of central government and the emperor, Kyoto saw many wars and conflicts. It was also a commercial centre while most of Japan remained agricultural (with the exception of Tokyo and Osaka). As a result, Kyoto people have gained a reputation for being shifty, always siding with the powerful, and changing sides without scruples for the purpose of their own survival. They are also said to be status conscious, never speaking their own minds, the masters of condescension, and looking down on outsiders without showing their true feelings. Very harsh, one must say, and it should be taken into account that these are the views of country folk who have been attracted by the bright lights of the ancient capital, but suffered some inevitable disappointments.

Without their conservative values and cunning, we would have lost Kyoto's old-fashioned charm. It's more than just ancient architecture – it is the city's entire atmosphere. The people of Kyoto have protected it against relentless and violent winds of change brought from outside, and there are always discussions about rolling back the modern and ugly effect of urbanisation throughout the city. We owe much to, and have a lot to thank for, Kyoto's 'character'.

Osaka 大阪

Osaka is located at the end of Seto Naikai (瀬戸内海), Japan's extensive inland sea, at the mouth of a river that connects it to Kyoto. It became a major city in the 15th century with the building of an important temple for Jōdo Buddhism, or Pure Land Buddhism. The temple flourished not only with the devotion of its followers, but also with the improvements it provided to the city and its port facilities.

During the Tokugawa shogunate, Osaka came under its direct control and developed into a commercial hub as envisaged by its successive conquerors. As feudal lords known as daimyō (大名) levied taxes on rice production, a large part of Japan's rice harvest found its way to Osaka to be converted into currency. Each feudal lord kept warehouses in Osaka, so local merchants flourished from the trade. Whilst the shogun ruled over Japan from Edo, Osaka's merchants dominated the marketplace and held the purse strings of the samurai.

The Tokugawa shogunate fell with the Meiji Reformation of 1868, but Osaka continued to thrive. Its commercial tradition meant it transitioned smoothly into modern capitalism, and the city attracted investment. Osaka was like a laboratory for a modern Japan. It was the first city to open department stores connected to train stations, a trend that would spread across Japan, and railway barons such as Ichizō Kobayashi (小林一三 1873–1957) connected the city centre with newly developed suburban residential areas. Kobayashi also developed a hot spring resort at the end of his railway line in Takarazuka (宝塚), and to attract even more visitors, he established an all-female theatre troupe called the Takarazuka Revue, which continues to be popular today.

Between March and August 1945, Osaka was destroyed by American carpet bombing, which took place eight times, resulting in more than 10,000 civilian fatalities. Like all of Japan's other cities, it got back on its feet quickly after the war.

In an homogenised Japan, Osakans are perhaps the only people who proudly speak with their own dialects – which have also become the language of the entertainment business, as Osaka was the birthplace of manzai (漫才), a form of conversational stand-up comedy which became sensationally popular in the 1980s.

Today, Osaka is losing ground in the ongoing economic competition with Tokyo. Many corporations previously based in Osaka have moved their headquarters to Tokyo, and for some time Osaka has had to settle for being second-best. Regardless, the city retains its culture and identity, and Japan counts on Osakans to keep things real by deflating the official lines coming out of Tokyo – continuing the tradition of those powerful merchants who kept the samurai on a leash.

日本の生き方

づぼらや
珍味てっちり
安心と信頼の日立グループ
新世界
日本一の串かつ 横綱
酒
広々としたお座敷もあります!!
大小宴会承り中
料理専門
9-22
9-22
1F カウンター席
2F 座敷あります

Tokyo 東京

Called Edo until the Meiji Reformation in 1868, Tokyo is a relatively new Japanese city. If you take a bus or taxi around Tokyo, you can see that it is built on an area that consisted of marshy swamps at the mouths of several major rivers that formed the plains of the Kantō region and flowed into Tokyo Bay. Many of the city's thoroughfares are built on covered-up small waterways and rivers which served as canals in the old days.

Edo started life in a similar way to Rome or Washington DC – its existence as a city relied solely on the fact that it was the seat of government, in this case the Tokugawa shogunate that existed between the 17th and 19th centuries.

The city is believed to have reached a population of 1 million by the beginning of the 18th century, but its rapid expansion was periodically halted by natural disasters. Flooding from heavy rainfalls and typhoons was disastrous for low-lying Edo. In addition, the initial lack of proper city planning made it vulnerable to great fires. To cap it all, earthquakes were (and, of course, still are) a major concern. In any event the native residents, known as *Edokko*, shrugged off the worries and chose to live in hope, rather than fear – a sentiment which has endured.

Edo's future seemed finished when the shogunate fell in the Meiji Reformation of 1868. However, the Meiji Emperor and his advisers decided to move the emperor's seat from Kyoto to Edo. At the same time, they also changed Edo's name to Tokyo, which means 'eastern capital'. The people of Kyoto are terribly unhappy about it to this day. As the capital city of a new Japan that espoused the values of Western civilisation, Tokyo continued to thrive. Commerce followed politics, and office buildings and suburbs started to spread beyond former boundaries.

Tokyo suffered terrible setbacks in the 20th century. The huge earthquake of 1923 caused almost 150,000 deaths and a massive amount of destruction. In 1944 and 1945, American bombing resulted in about 100,000 civilian casualties, with at least 1 million people displaced. Nevertheless Tokyo got back on its feet and started to rebuild. Today, the Tokyo Metropolis area boasts a population of over 13.5 million, and is still growing while Japan's national population level is decreasing.

One of the most iconic buildings of the modern city is Tokyo Tower, an orange-coloured Eiffel Tower-lookalike built in 1958. The 332.9m structure was built from the scrap steel of US tanks left behind after the Korean War. I love to point this out to American visitors, telling them, 'That's what peace can achieve'.

Even for a native like myself, Tokyo is an endlessly fascinating city. It has become enormous on the back of the rapid urbanisation that has taken place over the last 100 years. Today, it is trying to shift its focus to become an international global city, harnessing the energy coming from globalisation and Asia's meteoric growth. Many Britons say that London is not Britain. Americans may say that New York is not America. However, Tokyo will always be Japan and it will always lead, wherever Japan is heading.

Hokkaido 北海道

Hokkaido is the northernmost island of the Japanese archipelago, and is the home of the indigenous Ainu people (アイヌ), who settled there long before records began. The Ainu people resisted the cultural, political and racial amalgamation with the Japanese newcomers to the region – and their authority. In one such event, between 1669 and 1672, the Ainu rebelled against Japanese rule in an uprising known as Shakushain's Revolt (シャクシャインの戦い), named after the Ainu chieftain who led it.

Hokkaido furhter came to the attention of Japan's central government due to Imperial Russia's eastern expansion. The Tokugawa shogunate ordered a survey of Hokkaido in the late 18th century – except for the southern tip under the rule of the Kakizaki clan, the geographical details of the island were unknown. The map of Hokkaido was completed by Inō Tadataka (伊能忠敬1745–1818) in 1816, in a project that lasted some 16 years. The surveying expedition was met by their Russian counterparts at various points, marking the beginning of boundary disputes in these areas which continue today.

In the mid-19th century, the new government under the Meiji Reformation, continuing the policy of the Tokugawa shogunate, encouraged settlement in Hokkaido by subsidising pioneer farmers. As a result, peat marshes and barren landscapes were turned into farmland after much human endeavour. To this day it is known as a foodie hotspot, with the likes of the Sapporo brewery gaining much attention for their beer.

Due to a historical lack of government interference and its relatively recent agricultural development, Hokkaido has an outlook unlike the rest of Japan. Its vast open spaces and wide skies are very different from typical Japanese countryside scenery, and there is a true frontier air about it.

In the 1980s, a popular TV drama series began that spread that frontier image of Hokkaido to the rest of Japan. *Kita no kuni kara* (北の国から), or 'From the Northern Country', told the story of a farmer whose wife had left him and their two young children, struggling against the elements in Hokkaido. Many outside Hokkaido assumed this image of challenging terrain and hardship was accurate. So we were quite surprised when Australian and Chinese tourists turned that image of Hokkaido from a difficult frontier land into a powder-snow dreamland for skiers.

Kyūshū 九州

Kyūshū is one of the four major islands of the Japanese archipelago, and consists of seven prefectures: Fukuoka (福岡), Saga (佐賀), Nagasaki (長崎), Kumamoto (熊本), Ōita (大分), Miyazaki (宮崎) and Kagoshima (鹿児島).

The north of Kyūshū, principally Fukuoka and Nagasaki, has been Japan's gateway to the outside world, and is the closest point to continental Asia. Since the 7th century, the central government in Kyoto maintained the city of Dazaifu (太宰府) in present-day Fukuoka to deal with foreign affairs, and it hosted embassies for Korea and China.

Nagasaki, with its complex coastline not unlike Norway's *fjords*, provided ports for vessels and a haven for pirates who raided Chinese coastal areas between the 13th and 16th centuries. The Portuguese arrived in the mid-16th century, and Nagasaki became the hub for trade with Europe. After the Portuguese were banned from Japan for their Christian missionary work, the Dutch monopolised Japanese–European trade from the nearby artificial island of Dejima (出島) – the only point of contact with the outside world in the closed country era – until Japan opened up again in the mid-19th century. Early 20th-century Nagasaki is also the setting for Puccini's opera *Madama Butterfly*.

In contrast to the commercial and industrial areas, the rest of Kyūshū is generally rural, except for a number of factory towns. From its central region to the southern tip of Sakurajima (桜島) in Kagoshima, there are active volcanoes which provide the area with outstanding natural sights, *onsen* hot-spring resorts and occasional natural disturbances. The best known of Kyūshū's volcanoes are Mt Aso (阿蘇山) and Mt Sakurajima – both are still very active.

The city of Kagoshima, previously known as Satsuma (薩摩) – after which the citrus fruit was named – was one of the hotbeds for the revolutionaries who brought about the Meiji Reformation, and the volcanic activity of Sakurajima has forever been associated with the hot tempers of Kagoshima's citizens.

Tōhoku 東北

The Tōhoku region spreads to the north of the Kantō region and is divided into six prefectures: Aomori (青森), Iwate (岩手), Akita (秋田), Miyagi (宮城), Yamagata (山形) and Fukushima (福島). Tōhoku literally means 'northeastern'.

Ever since the establishment of central government in Kyoto in the 7th century, the sovereignty of the Tōhoku region was an ambiguous affair. The strength of its independence was supported by several factors. Firstly, Tōhoku people at that time retained stronger ties with indigenous people. Secondly, they had gold. You can still witness the legacy of this trade in the Konjiki-dō of Chūson-ji (中尊寺金色堂) – a golden hall in the well-known Buddhist temple, which is covered with gold leaf inside and out.

Tōhoku's independence was surrendered completely when the samurai of Kantō, united under their leader, Minamoto no Yoritomo (源頼朝 1147–1199), invaded Tōhoku in 1189 to bring the region under their rule. After the downfall of the Tokyrawa Shogunate, sporadic skirmishes continued, ending with a short, yet brutal resistance in 1868 and 1869. However, old wounds take time to heal – especially in a region known for long winters of heavy snowfall.

Today, Tōhoku is perhaps Japan's best-kept secret in terms of tourism. With breathtaking natural scenery, excellent sake breweries and fascinating ancient places of worship such as Dewa Sanzan (出羽三山 – the Three Mountains of Dewa), which have long flourished as pilgrimage destinations. Local festivals, such as the Aomori *Nebuta Matsuri* (青森ねぶた祭), Miyagi's Sendai *Tanabata Matsuri* (仙台七夕まつり), and the Akita Kantō *Matsuri* (秋田竿灯まつり), are spectacular. You can also see samurai on horseback in full gallop at Fukushima's Soma-Nomaoi (相馬野馬追).

The love and pride that the people of Tōhoku hold for their region is so passionate and sincere that it is almost contagious – which makes Fukushima's nuclear disaster in 2011 all the more tragic. While the situation is fortunately contained, it will take a long time to heal. The diligence and resilience of those who work on the long mission of containment is yet another testament to the spirit of the people.

日本の生き方

Okinawa 沖縄

Okinawa is the largest island in a chain of the islands that create a 'dotted line' between the Japanese archipelago and Taiwan. The prefecture, also called Okinawa, is vast – the distance between its northernmost and southernmost points is about 400km, and from the easternmost to the westernmost, about 1,000km. That area is, of course, mostly ocean, and 90 percent of its approximately 1.5m population live on the main island.

The climate is tropical, the beaches beautiful, and the coral reefs endlessly inviting. In short, except for some nasty typhoons that make regular visits along the island chain, it is a paradise. However, history has been unkind to this idyll.

In the 15th century, the various clans of the islands were unified under a king, Shō Hashi (尚巴志 c.1371–1439). The kingdom of Ryukyu, as it was known, flourished as an intermediary trade port between Japan and China. To maintain the trading relationship, Okinawa remained a loosely tied tributary state of the reigning Chinese Ming dynasty.

At the beginning of Tokugawa shogunate, the warlord of Satsuma invaded Okinawa as a show of force. The conflict was brief and one-sided. The end result was that Okinawa became a dual tributary state to Japan as well as China, with Satsuma controlling the intermediary trade passing through Okinawa. China under the Qing dynasty (1636–1911) was somewhat indifferent to overseas matters, and as Satsuma's economic grip on Okinawa was harsh and strong, it shifted closer to Japan. Eventually, the full annexation of Okinawa ended its independent past, but brought modernisation to the islands.

During the Second World War, Okinawa was one of the fiercest battlefields in the Pacific theatre. Operation Iceberg commenced on 1st April 1945, with about 550,000 American and British soldiers making an amphibious attack on Okinawa Island, which was defended by about 116,000 Japanese soldiers. It ended three months later with about 180,000 Japanese deaths, half of which were civilian.

The Okinawan islands were put under American rule after the war, and remained so for nearly 30 years until 1972, when the area returned to Japan. However, the Americans remained, and Okinawa became the US base for the later Korean (1950–1953) and Vietnam (1955–1975) wars. With about 15 percent of Okinawa Island still occupied by US military today, and about 26,000 service members stationed there, Okinawans understandably wish to ease tensions in the region.

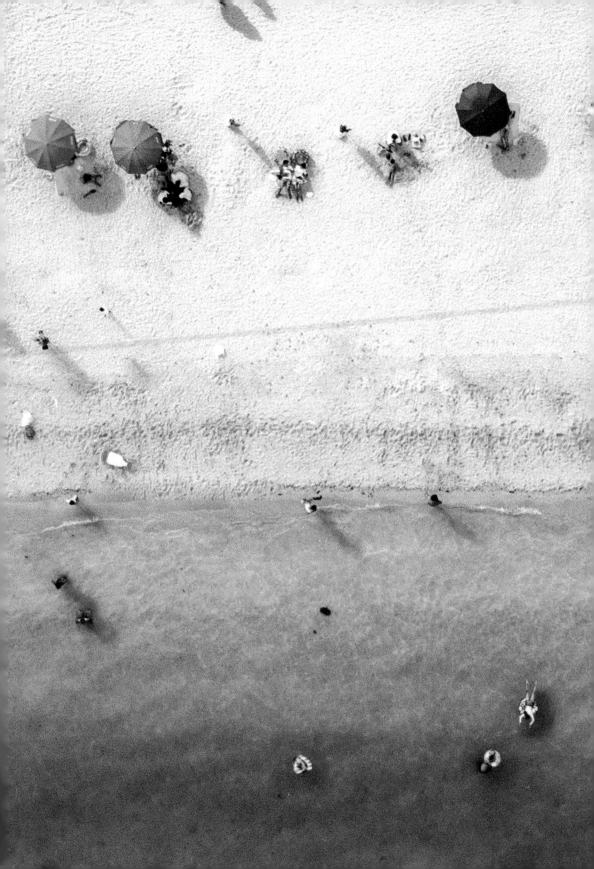

Tōkai 東海地方

The Tōkai region consists of the prefectures of Aichi (愛知), Gifu (岐阜), Mie (三重) and Shizuoka (静岡). Apart from landlocked Gifu, all face the Pacific Ocean.

Tōkai (東海) means 'eastern sea', and comes from the name for the ancient Tōkaidō coastal route (東海道 – 'eastern sea route') that stretched out of Kyoto towards Edo.

There is a ferry crossing from Ise (伊勢) in Mie to the area near what is now Nagoya (名古屋), the biggest city in the region. Ise is known for the Ise-Jingū (伊勢神宮), the mother of all Shinto shrines, dedicated to the sun goddess Amaterasu, and worshipped since time immemorial.

Nagoya, on the other hand, is of recent vintage. At the mouth of three rivers running from the mountains of the Japanese Alps, it is built on swampland made habitable after extensive flood control works in the 17th century. Nagoya's citizens get a lot of stick from both Tokyo and Kansai for being in the middle of Japan, and neither west nor east. It is unofficially known as 'Toyota town', as the car manufacturing giant has its headquarters nearby. Some say Nagoya's streets are so wide because Toyota insisted on it. That's unlikely to be true, unless Toyota once wanted to make American-style large cars – which they never did.

Shizuoka is geographically wide. It stretches for 155km between its easternmost and westernmost points. When you take the motorway from Tokyo to Nagoya or beyond, the sight of Mt Fuji standing so majestically to the north as you approach Shizuoka through the pass in the mountains is very exciting. Then you realise the road just goes on and on along the sea coast, and you are still in Shizuoka. By the time you lose sight of Mt Fuji, you are grateful for its disappearance.

At first glance, Shizuoka looks very rural. It is actually home to some world-famous motorbike manufacturers such as Honda, Yamaha and Suzuki. Yamaha began as a manufacturer of musical instruments and continues to sell them today, and its rival piano-maker Kawai is also based in Shizuoka.

Tōkai is blessed with a sunny climate, and as a result, it is famous for tea, oranges and eels. Nagoya is famous for *hitsumabushi*, its grilled eel on rice. Personally, I do not think much of it. As a Tokyo native, I naturally feel our way is the best.

The region is named after a thoroughfare, and I think it suffers from the toll booth attendant's lament: everybody is going somewhere, except you.

日本の生き方

Chūgoku 中国

The Chūgoku region lies to the west of Kansai. It looks a bit like a tailbone attached to the biggest island of the Japanese archipelago, Honshū (本州). It consists of five different prefectures – Tottori (鳥取), Shimane (島根), Okayama (岡山), Hiroshima (広島), and Yamaguchi (山口).

The region is divided down the middle by a mountain range that stretches from east to west. As a result, the south and the north of this area have very different outlooks.

The southern prefectures of Okayama and Hiroshima face the inland sea of Setonaikai. The northern prefectures of Tottori and Shimane face the comparatively rougher Sea of Japan. Yamaguchi prefecture, and the city of Shimonoseki (下関) at the westernmost tip, flourished as a toll collector for ships passing from the outer waters into Setonaikai and vice versa.

Yamaguchi was known as Chōshū (長州) in the Edo era, and together with Satsuma, was the main feudal fiefdom that brought down the Tokugawa shogunate. As such, it has a long political tradition going back to the Meiji Reformation. Japan's prime minister, at the time of writing, Shinzō Abe (安倍晋三) and his family are from Yamaguchi.

The city of Hiroshima is the biggest in the region. Sadly, it is known internationally for being one of the two cities destroyed by atomic bombs during the Second World War (together with the city of Nagasaki). The main reason for Hiroshima being targeted was that it served the major naval port of Kure (呉) nearby. Hiroshima has thrived on shipbuilding and shipping industries, and is also the home to the carmaker Mazda.

Okayama is probably the most benign region of Japan. Historically, it has had the least number of typhoons and earthquakes than anywhere else in Japan. Okayama is also home to the picturesque city of Kurashiki (倉敷), with its rows of old Japanese-style warehouses – another testament to the region's shipping legacy.

Tottori and Shimane are somewhat isolated prefectures. In ancient times, however, they were important as they are close to the continental mainland. Izumo (出雲), in Shimane, is where the Izumo-taisha shrine (出雲大社) is located (its official name is *Izumo Ōyashiro*). It is dedicated to *Ōkuninushi* (大国主大神).

Shimane was also known for its Iwami Ginzan (石見銀山) silver mine. In the 16th and 17th centuries, Japan is said to have produced one third of the world's silver, and most of it came from this mine alone. For eager panhandlers, I must warn you that the mine has now ceased production and is closed. Nevertheless, the name of Iwami was noted in the primitive map of Asia made by the Jesuits, who were as eager for worldly wealth as they were for religious converts, whether they were in Peru or Japan.

Tottori is the least populous prefecture of Japan. At one point, it had the honour of being the only prefecture without a Starbucks, but had to surrender that title in 2015 when a branch opened. Tottori is known for its large sand dunes, Tottori *sakyu* (鳥取砂丘), which stretch for 16km of coastline.

Shikoku 四国

Shikoku is the smallest of the four major islands of the Japanese archipelago. It fits in like a jigsaw piece at the spot cornered by the western tail of Honshū and Kyūshū islands, with its southern edge facing the Pacific Ocean. Shikoku literally means 'four regions'. True to its name, it consists of the four prefectures of Tokushima (徳島県), Kagawa (香川県), Ehime (愛媛県) and Kōchi (高知県).

Historically, Shikoku has been the place to where those of high rank were exiled. Although it only takes a little over three hours by car from Kyoto to Kagawa today, it was regarded as a world apart by the blue-blooded of the past, with their sedate and diabetes-inducing lifestyles.

Kagawa is, in fact, a lovely, sunny place, and the birthplace of Kūkai (空海 774–835), the well-known leader of early Buddhism in Japan. The place is renowned for its *udon* noodles (うどん), which are made from wheat flour. *Sanuki* (讃岐), the old name for Kagawa, is synonymous with the noodle throughout Japan.

Tokushima lies at the eastern tip of Shikoku island and faces the strait that connects the Pacific Ocean to the internal sea of Setonaikai. The ebb and flow of the current between these bodies of water creates a famous whirlpool off the coast of Tokushima, known as *Naruto no Uzushio* (鳴門の渦潮). Fishing is an important industry for the region, and it is well regarded for producing delicious snapper – it is said that Tokushima's snapper have to swim against the strong current, making their meat that much tastier.

Ehime is located in the north-western corner of the island, and its coastal towns and islands once provided bases for the pirates that controlled the internal sea lane until the end of the Warring States era that lasted between the 15th and 17th centuries. The place is warm and sunny, and known for producing various citrus fruits, especially *mikan* (みかん), more popularly known in the English-speaking world as tangerines. They are usually harvested in November and December and for centuries have been a vital source of vitamin C during winter months.

Kōchi stretches along the whole southern coast of Shikoku island and faces the Pacific Ocean. Whilst Shikoku was regarded as a land of exiles, Kōchi was regarded as the destination for the exiles of the exiled. It is best known for Sakamoto Ryōma (坂本龍馬 1836–1867), the famous revolutionary of the period leading up to the Meiji Reformation, who organised Japan's first modern, private merchant-navy company. His life was immortalised in a hugely popular novel, *Ryōma ga Yuku* (竜馬がゆく *Ryōma Goes His Way*) by Ryōtarō Shiba (司馬遼太郎1923–1996), first serialised in the *Sankei Shimbun* (産経新聞) newspaper in 1962. Shiba's portrayal of Sakamoto became so popular and influential that there are still pilgrims who visit Sakamoto's enormous statue by the beach in Kōchi.

日本の生き方

Kii Peninsula and other 'Power Spots'

A recent trend in Japanese domestic tourism is visiting what are called 'Power Spots' – locations that people believe to be auspicious for historical significance or natural beauty. The visitors are, presumably, blessed with good karma by seeing these places.

Perhaps one of the most popular destinations for Power Spot tourism is the Kii Peninsula (紀伊半島), on the island of Honshū. It spreads to the south of Osaka and Nara, and sticks out into the Pacific Ocean like a pregnant woman's belly. It is believed to have been created by huge accient volcanoes, and it sits on a fault line.

Kii is close to the political centres such as Nara and Kyoto, but is so dense with rainforest wilderness and crease after crease of mountain ranges that it was a natural destination for fugitives. Emperor Jimmu (神武天皇), the legendary first emperor of Japan, is said to have been repelled by those who occupied Nara so he sailed around the Kii peninsula and re-landed where the present-day town of Kumano stands and marched back onto Nara to claim victory.

The ancient roads from Kumano have become pilgrimage routes and are recognised as a UNESCO World Heritage Site.

Mt Fuji is another obvious 'Power Spot' destination, although it is inadvisable to attempt an ascent without proper planning and training. Yakushima Island (屋久島) in the southern tip of Kyūshū, with its wild rainforest and veteran cedar trees, is also very popular. The ancient capital of Nara also attracts many 'Power Spot' enthusiasts, as they believe, rather tenuously, that having been a capital city, there must have been some mysterious powers there. There are also several not-so-high mountains in Nara which are believed to be divine.

For those who cannot travel far from Tokyo, there is a famous 'Power Spot' in the middle of the city's business district. Masakado no Kubizuka (将門の首塚) is believed to be the spot where the severed head of a 10th-century samurai rebel is said to be buried. Taira no Masakado (平将門 died 940) was a local chief who conquered the whole of the Kantō region and declared himself a new emperor. He was killed in battle and his head was cut from his body to be displayed in Kyoto. Legend has it that the head flew across the sky like a rocket and landed on the spot upon which Masakado-zuka, literally meaning 'Masakado's mound', stands today.

As it is right at the heart of the business district, several attempts have been made to remove this historical site to make way for development. Each attempt has been met with some disaster or another, so people started to believe that the spot is protected by a strong occult power. It is said to bring luck to pay a visit to Masakado-zuka before making a long trip. They say that Masakado's spirit ensures you will return safely. In one piece, one hopes, and not just your head.

Kōshin'etsu 甲信越

Kōshin'etsu (甲信越) is a subregion based on the old names of three prefectures: Kai (甲斐), Shinano (信濃), and Echigo (越後). The name 'Kōshin'etsu' takes the first Chinese character of each, 'Kō (甲)', 'Shin (信)' and 'Etsu (越)'.

They are geographically large prefectures, but are mostly mountainous, and habitable land is very limited. Yamanashi basically consists of a basin surrounded by mountain ranges to the north, east and west, with its south side sealed by the colossal Mt Fuji. Due to this geography, massive snowfall in 2014 resulted in Yamanshi being cut off from the outside world. In a true demonstration of Japanese spirit, most major supermarket and convenience store chains took up the challenge posed by the natural calamity and competed to keep their shops open, mobilising helicopters to airlift merchandise despite the logistical difficulties. Yamanashi's soil is not naturally fertile and, as a result, its agriculture has traditionally excelled at value-added products such as fruit and, more recently, wine. From spring to autumn, farmers open their orchards for weekend tourists to pick their own strawberries, peaches and pears, as their harvesting seasons arrive.

Nagano is sandwiched between the Hida and Akaishi mountain ranges. Its major cities and towns are dotted along the River Shinano, which runs through it. There is a long distance from north to south. The distance and hilly landscape prevent the mixing of people from each area within Nagano, and they are famous for proudly holding on to their home places. Nagano was the host of the 1998 Winter Olympics, and is rightly famous for its ski resorts, combined with excellent hot spas. Shredding the slopes of mountains that rise to blue sky like frozen white flames is truly breathtaking. Like Yamanashi, Nagano is also into value-added agricultural products, with apples that are rightly prized for their juiciness. Chestnut sweets from the village of Obuse (小布施) are also a big deal.

Nīgata arches to the north, facing the Sea of Japan. Unlike Yamanashi or Nagano, Nīgata is a fertile place, with several rivers running through the land to the sea. With the ease of irrigation, Nīgata has become one of the top prefectures for rice production. Rice grown in the Uonuma (魚沼) area of Niigata has consistently won prizes, and is known throughout Japan. With good rice and quality water, Nīgata is also teeming with sake brewers – cold winter months favour the brewing process. The area includes Sado Island (佐渡ヶ島), which floats in the Sea of Japan just off the coast. Gold was discovered in Sado at the beginning of 17th century, and its prolific production (at its peak, it produced around 400kg of gold per year) contributed to its economic stability throughout the Edo era. Production ceased in 1989.

日本の生き方

What Makes
the Japanese

Geography and people

Japanese people believe in climate change. If the sea levels hadn't risen to submerge the land and separate continental Asia from the archipelago that would become Japan, you would still be able to walk from Korea to Japan. Indeed, you could still walk from China to Korea. You don't need a PhD in international relations to see the significance: geography creates history. But does geography define people?

Japan lies at the north-western corner of what is known as the Ring of Fire, the rim of the Pacific Ocean which experiences frequent earthquakes and volcanic eruptions as colliding tectonic plates slide deep into the underwater abyss. Japan is on top of the boundaries between *four* tectonic plates. It is the geoscientific equivalent of Tokyo's Shibuya Crossing or a particularly belligerent corner of a spotty teenager's face. While Japan's active volcanoes and frequent earthquakes are challenging to say the least, these unique geological features have also blessed us with natural hot spas dotted across the country.

Weather-wise, Japan presents varying faces, from harsh winters in the northernmost Hokkaido, to the seemingly everlasting summer of Okinawa in the south. Nevertheless, we have one thing in common. Sandwiched between the continental weather system over the Asian mainland, and the oceanic system over the Pacific, Japan's weather is constantly changing; we are famously exposed to gale-force typhoons, mainly just after the summer heat.

We have come to expect sudden and often violent climatic changes happening with very little foreshadowing. A.O. Scott, a film critic for the *New York Times*, once said that Godzilla, the Japanese fictional monster, is the epitome of our reverence for the natural force that is beyond human control or comprehension. I think he hit the nail on the head. Ultimately, nature cannot be tamed. In our fear and reverence for it, we have become fatalistic.

On the other hand, we have also learnt to enjoy the lulls between natural catastrophes. A life spent in fear is not a life well lived. In this sense, we have become pleasure-seeking and sensuous.

日
本
の
生
き
方

Women

'In the beginning, woman was the sun.'

Raichō HIRATSUKA (平塚 らいちょう 1886–1971), Japan's pioneering feminist.

One of the more striking features of Japanese society in what is called the early classical period between the 6th and 8th centuries is the ease with which a female ruler was accepted. In fact, during the 7th and 8th centuries, immediately prior to and following the coup of 645, Japan saw six empresses on the throne, reigning for more than 80 years in total.

Even in the early historical era, Japan was known to have female rulers. The earliest record of this comes from the official chronicle of the Chinese Wei Dynasty from between 220-265 (written sometime between 280 and 297). In it, Japan is described as a loose confederation of nations headed by the largest of them, Yamatai (or Yamato), and ruled by a shamanistic queen called Himiko. She was succeeded by an unsuccessful male king, who caused wars over the succession. That turbulent period was brought to an end by the ascension of Himiko's daughter, Toyo (also known as Iyo), as the queen and overlord.

The Chinese account also mentions that the Japanese had tattooed faces, drank a lot (plus ça change) and, while society was not promiscuous, even a poor man had two or three wives. Against this polygynous social background, it is surprising that the ancient Japanese still accepted a female ruler.

It was probably believed and accepted by the ancient Japanese that female rulers had closer links with the gods than the male ones, even if their reigns entailed increased likelihood of succession problems, much like England's 'Virgin Queen', Elizabeth I.

The authors of the first official history of Japan had little difficulty recognising that the supreme deity in the native pantheon was female, because of the ancient memories of female spiritual leaders, as well as the presence of more recent female rulers. Under the circumstances, it was natural for them to declare that the imperial family had descended from the sun goddess, Amaterasu.

After nearly 700 years of government by the samurai, during which the emperors and empresses had been restricted to a merely symbolic role, a martial figure emerged in 1867: Emperor Meiji. This was intentional. To compete with Western imperialism, photographs of the emperor sporting a moustache and wearing a braided military tunic were thrust upon the Japanese people. We are still living in the shadow of this hyper-masculine image, which is a relatively modern fabrication.

Given the historical background, it is more than ironic that lawmakers are *still* arguing about whether or not to allow women to accede to today's Chrysanthemum throne.

In the beginning…

Japan was first organised as a loose confederation of clans under the figurehead of an emperor or empress, and was finally brought together by a coup in 645, led by a prince, Naka-no-Ōe no-Ōji (中大兄皇子). The centralised national government realised it needed to bring together the numerous clan chiefs spread across the archipelago, who were mainly based in enclaves divided by the seas and mountain ranges, and who governed through complicated networks of alliances. A belief system in the form of shared stories, myths and legends was needed: a history.

The new imperial government recognised this spiritual side to their nation-building efforts. It was also thought that such an official history would bring legitimacy to the regime. The imperial family, now operating under the new philosophy, published two historical books: *Kojiki* (古事記 – *Records of Ancient Matters*) and *Nihon Shoki* (日本書紀 – *The Chronicles of Japan*). Both are probably the oldest books in existence in Japan. They are essentially anthologies of ancient stories which had come down the generations orally, maintained by professional storytellers who memorised the tales. Of course, the editors of *Kojiki* and *Nihon Shoki* did more than just write down the old stories. They *edited* the collections, from the creation myths to the immediate past, so they aligned with the ideals of the imperial lineage and its legitimacy to rule over Japan.

The official 'history' says that the Imperial Family are the descendants of the sun goddess Amaterasu (天照), one of the highest deities in Shintoism. They and their followers, *amatsu-kami* (天津神), or the 'heavenly gods', arrived from the celestial place to the land that is Japan, but did not find the place empty. It was occupied by the *kunitsu-kami* (国津神), gods living on earth, whose leader is known, among many other names, as Ōkuninushi (大国主).

The initial expeditions seem to have gone awry, with the invaders being seduced by aboriginal sirens and going native. After several attempts and some conflict, one of which tells the tale of the first sumo match between two braves each representing his side, Ōkuninushi finally concedes sovereignty to the goddess Amaterasu and her *amatsu-kami* on the condition that they build him the biggest shrine in the land. *Izumo-taisha* still stands today.

Ōkuninushi's concession of sovereignty is depicted as a peaceful negotiation with minimum violence. There is also the myth of Sarutahiko (猿田彦). He was a *kunitsu-kami* who awaited the invading force of amatsu-kami at a crossroads. Sarutahiko had a big nose and glaring eyes, features which were so alien from those of the *amatsu-kami*. To ascertain whether Sarutahiko was friend or foe, the goddess Amaterasu sent the dance goddess Ame-no-Uzume (天宇受売命), to negotiate with him. Ame-no-Uzume interpreted her instructions in the widest possible terms, and seduced Sarutahiko – whereupon he offered to act as a guide for the newcomers. Sarutahiko, a *kunitsu-kami*, and Ame-no-Uzume, an *amatsu-kami*, became husband and wife, and gods of roads (道祖神). You can still see their pint-size shrines by roadsides, if you know where to look.

日
本
の
生
き
方

Spirituality

The introduction of Buddhism to Japan was very much a 'top-down' affair. It was an imported religion of immigrant technocrats, officially adopted by the emperor, who was aided and abetted by powerful factions in the governing elites.

The first wave of Buddhism reached its zenith in 752 with the building of a giant Buddha statue at Tōdai-ji (東大寺), in the then capital city of Nara (奈良). It is made of bronze, measures around 16m in height, and weighs in at a whopping 250 tons. Emperor Shōmu (聖武天皇701–756) was a fervent believer, and ordered the construction of the giant Buddha as an act of appeasement in the hope of alleviating a smallpox epidemic and halting the natural disasters which blighted Japan during his reign. He also ordered the construction of a Buddhist temple in each of the provinces throughout his realm. However, this had more to do with efficient taxation for a massive construction project in the capital city than evangelism. Buddhism had more to do with filling the government coffers than saving souls at that time.

To fill the spiritual void, the Japanese had to wait for Kūkai (空海 774–835). The son of a minor nobleman of the aristocratic Saeki family, in Buddhism he sought spiritual fulfilment, rather than just knowledge. Kūkai managed to squeeze himself into the government's diplomatic mission to Tang China in 804 as an official student. There, he studied Vajrayāna, also known as Tantric Buddhism, which was the latest trend in Buddhist teaching. He was instructed by Huiguo (惠果746–805), a Chinese monk who was the foremost authority on the subject.

Kūkai returned to Japan in 806, and the country soon went crazy for the Good News of Tantric Buddhism. It required faith to study and believe in the Buddhist Tantras, and to recite exotic-sounding utterances (mantras) in Sanskrit as the way to attain Nirvana. Faith had been missing from Japanese Buddhism until this point.

Faith is a great leveller. It is not the privilege of the elites; ordinary people can have faith in the same way as aristocrats, even emperors. Thus, Buddhism started on the path to popularisation in Japan.

As Buddhism broke class barriers, a strange phenomenon started to happen in Japan's spiritual landscape: the people started to merge Shinto gods into Buddhism's theological context. They basically promoted all their various local gods into the new popular religion. The Shinto gods became, if not 'The Enlightened One', then at least sidekicks of The Enlightened One, with varying classifications in accordance with the Buddhist hierarchy attached to them. People started to worship Shinto gods alongside Buddha. Temples and shrines merged, and deities coexisted alongside each other in a weirdly comfortable way within Japanese spirituality. This trend continued until the Meiji Reformation. As the emperors were deemed the descendants of the sun goddess, the promiscuous mixing of Shinto gods with Indian deities became a bit of a theological embarrassment at a time when the role of emperor as the head of state came under the spotlight.

日
本
の
生
き
方

Zen Buddhism was another import from China, and centred on the teaching of meditation as the way to attain Nirvana. It became the religion for the new Samurai elites during the 12th century, at a time when the popularisation of Buddhism was steadily advancing. The life of ordinary people improved during the Kamakura period (12th–14th century), with advancement in agricultural methods and an increase in commerce aided by the adoption of currency. The ordinary people, unlike the stoic samurai, sought a little more from their religion than sitting down. As a result, Jodo Buddhism (浄土仏教), or Pure Land Buddhism, gained popularity, which promises salvation in return for devotion though reciting of mantra, as did Nichiren Buddhism (日蓮宗), started by a monk called Nichiren (日蓮1222–1282), which teaches salvation through devotion to the Lotus Sutra.

In the Age of Warring States (c.1467–c.1603), certain temples and religious groups gained considerable political and military power, and became forces to be reckoned with. Into this crucible of religious beliefs, the Jesuits made landfall with Christianity in the 1540s. They soon found devout followers among both the poor and the rich and powerful. Their religion taught equality before God. The subversive doctrine of equality was always powerful and had been a common theme in all the religious beliefs which had come before, but this time it was stronger. The Jesuits' message of salvation was front and centre. When the persecution of Christians happened in the late 16th and early 17th centuries, they did not lack for martyrs.

When Tokugawa Ieyasu (徳川家康1543–1616) became the first shōgun of Tokugawa in 1603, he was keenly aware of the need to contain religious zealots if peace was to be maintained. He ordered that everybody register with a temple of their choice by way of registering their citizenship – in effect, delegating civil administration powers to religious establishments. As an arm of governmental authority, the temples gained a steady source of income and lost their zeal for converting people.

Two hundred and fifty years of peace ensued. Nothing saps religious fervour like apathy nurtured in peaceful prosperity.

This irreligiosity continues to this day. Visitors to Japan today are often confused by the apparent lack of scruples in our religious practices. We claim to be Buddhists, but marry in Christian churches, celebrate Christmas, and welcome in the New Year at Shinto shrines. They may conclude that we are not religious, and they may have a point. It has not always been thus. People believed, and they did so deeply. If I could hazard a guess, our apparent nonchalance is only skin-deep, disguised by our tendency to subscribe to an 'every little helps' attitude when it comes to seeking supernatural intervention, and a preference of practical solutions over dogmatic inconveniences in the matter of faith. This can be seen from our merging of Buddhism and Shinto in the early days.

When Emperor Meiji died, there was a surge in the number of Catholics in Japan. He had been the symbol of modernising Japan and presided over unprecedented societal changes. When he was gone, people felt insecure and sought spiritual support. Everybody has a reason to believe. Even the Japanese.

The Emperor

The Emperor and his household are an enigma. The legend, first introduced in the 7th century and revived with gusto during the Meiji Restoration and in the run-up to the Second World War, is that the imperial linage goes all the way back to Emperor Jimmu, whose reign is supposed to have started in 660 BC. This is almost certainly a myth. That said, the lineage *does* go back to time immemorial, where written records are scarce (for one thing, the Japanese didn't have a writing system then). The official historical record from China's Three Kingdoms era (220–280 AD) notes that there was a series of kings and queens ruling the islands to the east – Japan.

At the time of the Meiji Restoration, it was a bit of a hard sell to reinstate the authority of an emperor. Ever since being sidelined by the government samurai in the 12th century, emperors have been regarded as a relic of an ancient era. It was a minor miracle that they have lasted at all. After 250 years of the Tokugawa shogunate's rigid grip on power, uniting the country under imperial authority was an idea cherished only by a number of revolutionaries, merely as a counter to the shōgun's authority. But it worked. Much effort was spent to revitalise the idea of an emperor as head of state. It went into overdrive in the early 1940s, when politicians and military leaders felt the need to unite a country at war. (That was because they had put the country under enormous stress in the first place, but that is another story.)

Following defeat in 1945, the role of the Emperor came under scrutiny. As the head of state, Emperor Hirohito's role in, and responsibility for, the war was impossible to deny. Still, the American conquerors were surprised to discover how little power Emperor Hirohito yielded in reality. Given the potential havoc to be expected as a result of the abolition of the emperor, and the fact that he played a big role in pacifying and uniting the war-torn Japanese immediately after the war, the position of emperor remained. His ancient mission to 'respect harmony' saved the tradition. Hirohito died in 1989, and is now referred to as Emperor Shōwa, named after the period in which he reigned.

Under the current constitution, the emperor's position is said to be based on the nation's consensus. Republicans argue that there is no such consensus. However, faced with the ghastly prospect of alternative arrangements, it is fair to say that the role is secured on the basis of the nation's acquiescence.

For official courtly engagements such as annual rituals, weddings, and so on, members of the Imperial Family dress in costume from the Heian period (平安時代 794–1185), when the power of the household and its courtiers was paramount. They have also revived some charmingly quaint ancient customs, such as the reigning Emperor Akihito (明仁) planting rice by hand, a ritual for wishing a good harvest. His wife, Empress Michiko (美智子), performs a similar ritual where she cares for silkworms. They host the annual *Utakai Hajime* (歌会始), a traditional poetry reading event in early January. Anyone can enter the event by submitting their own opus in the hope of being selected as the author to be presented to the Emperor and have his or her own poem read

日
本
の
生
き
方

out loud. Japanese people enjoy such benign gestures that connect us to our unique history, tradition and culture.

Though they may have been the head of a Korean invading horde at some point beyond the mists of ancient history, the imperial household is not descended from some *parvenu* Normans of questionable parentage, or *arriviste* provincial German noblemen – that we know for sure! After nearly two millennia of lineage, we have long passed the genealogical optimal point, which means that almost all Japanese are related to the imperial household in one way or another. Besides, revolution is so anti-harmony.

Samurai

The Battle of Baekgang in 663 AD was a disaster for Japan. The Emperor had tried to revive the dynasty of Baekje on the Korean Peninsula against the allied forces of the (what would now be Korean) Silla dynasty and Tang dynasty of China. Japan lost badly, and following the defeat, the Emperor refrained from foreign wars. Once the threat of retaliation had waned, and public finances became a pressing issue, Japan decided to abandon the standing army. The loss of the military arm of central government meant the absence of any policing force. Left to their own devices, farmers everywhere in Japan had to arm themselves for self-defence against outlaws. This was the beginning of the samurai.

While early samurai were to be found throughout Japan, the Kantō region, a flat (and at that stage, wet and marshy) area around present-day Tokyo, became the legendary birthplace of super-warriors known as *bando musha* (坂東武者), or 'Warriors of the East'.

In those times, Kantō formed the eastern border of the government in Kyoto. Beyond the region, to the north, were the lands belonging to the indigenous peoples whose allegiances to the emperor's authority were, at best, shifty. Minor skirmishes between the farmers of Kantō and marauding northerners were frequent. At times, the central government announced punitive campaigns to the north. In the absence of a standing army, the emperor's general was forced to travel to Kantō only with his own private retinue, and then hire local warriors as mercenaries. All these circumstances provided ample opportunities for training, and many of the warriors excelled in martial skills.

The situation is somewhat similar to the Wild West of America: an agricultural lifestyle interspersed with armed conflicts with the indigenous peoples or to settle boundary disputes with neighbours. The difference is that samurai did not wield firearms. Their choice of weapon was horseback archery. True, the Japanese produced magnificent swords, and continue to do so, but in practical fighting, nothing at that time could better the rapid hit-and-run of arrow shots from the back of a horse. Today, you can witness the mastery of this art, now known as *yabusame* (流鏑馬), by modern-day practitioners at festivals across Japan. Samurai prided themselves on their accuracy when firing arrows from the horse at full gallop, and it certainly is a sight to behold.

Eventually, samurai developed their own ethics and code of honour for, and among, themselves. Like the American cowboys, they valued masculine qualities such as physical bravery, strength, loyalty, camaraderie, and manly outdoor pursuits like hunting. On the other hand, they abhorred cowardice, treachery and anything deemed effeminate. As history unfolded and society developed, the social mores of samurai changed, and their system of values became more complex.

Wabi-sabi

The Age of Warring States had a significant impact. Far beyond the usual standard historical facts of who won which battle and the political consequences thereof, the constant state of warfare for nearly 150 years left an indelible mark on the Japanese psyche, which manifested itself in a cultural and philosophical metamorphosis.

To grasp the topsy-turvy nature of the era, it's important to know that at the end of the era, Japan's leader was Toyotomi Hideyoshi (豊臣秀吉1537–1598). He had been born a peasant and risen to the top to unify the country. He ordered the invasion of mainland Asia, bringing war to Korea. Japan is said to have possessed the biggest firepower in the world by the end of the period.

Like Europe, where civilisation developed at breakneck speed through the constant warfare of the 16th–18th centuries, Japan went through an unprecedented transformation. To support the constant war effort, which became increasingly more expensive, warlords encouraged the development of local commerce. Commercial cities, such as Sakai (堺), near present-day Osaka, flourished. The powerful needed the rich. In turn and by necessity, the powerful became rich themselves. In the end, Japan had a handful of rich and powerful warlords and their lieutenant samurai who found themselves as the new leaders of unified Japan.

Unfortunately, they were an uncultured lot. Literacy was low among fighting men and they were generally quite uncouth. At the same time, the long absence of central authority created a fissure in Japanese cultural tradition. The new leaders had to find new traditions.

The art of the tea ceremony provided the focal point for newly minted political and economic leaders seeking status and common cultural experience. It started among wealthy merchants in places like Sakai. Sen no Rikyū, that greatest of tea ceremony masters, was a merchant of Sakai who is said to have traded in – rather tellingly, and among other goods – gunpowder. The tea ceremony was quickly picked up by the warlords and became fashionable. Soon, they were competing for the ownership of artefacts necessary to enrich their tea ceremony experiences, such as pottery, paintings and other paraphernalia.

Characteristically, Hideyoshi went to an extreme. He famously created a tea ceremony room in his residence which was made of gold, in an ostentatious show of his power and wealth. His tea ceremony was filled with exquisite porcelain imported from China.

Rikyū was Hideyoshi's instructor in the art of the tea ceremony, but frowned on his master's nouveau-riche tastes. In a brave artistic protest, Rikyū proposed new aesthetics to be observed in his style of tea ceremony, which were the opposite of Hideyoshi's ostentatious extravagances.

Rikyū called his aesthetic philosophy *wabi* (侘び) and *sabi* (寂び). *Wabi* refers to modest circumstances. Rikyū encouraged his followers to seek quiet satisfaction in less than opulent surroundings, and to find beauty in the modest beauty that shines more in contrast to its seemingly shabby environment. *Sabi* refers to internal quiet and peace. Rikyū proposed that true appreciation of beauty is borne out of the person's quiet contentment, rather than avarice.

The uncultured and somewhat barbaric samurai warriors, who possessed shaky intellect in search of status, were now enlightened as to the true value of artistic beauty in the new era.

In turn, Rikyū's philosophy of *wabi-sabi* formed the new basis on which Japanese culture was to flourish all the way to the present day.

Rikyū's artistic stand against Hideyoshi earned him the overlord's wrath for what the latter deemed was impertinence. In the end, Hideyoshi ordered Rikyū either to seek his forgiveness, or to commit suicide by way of punishment. Rikyū remained true to his belief and chose to take his own life. As a result, he was immortalised forever.

Wabi-sabi remains the cornerstone of the Japanese aesthetic. After centuries of warfare, the Japanese rejected in Hideyoshi our version of France's Sun King and his Versailles-like golden tea room. We continued to seek private happiness and contentment in the modesty and quietness which are, with a little effort, available to all, not just the rich and powerful.

Ikigai

A JAPANESE CONCEPT MEANING A REASON FOR BEING

Satisfaction but feeling of uselessness

Delight and fullness, but no wealth

What you **LOVE**

PASSION

MISSION

What you are **GOOD AT**

Ikigai

What the world **NEEDS**

PROFESSION

VOCATION

Comfortable, but feeling of emptiness

What you can be **PAID FOR**

Excitement and complacency but sense of uncertainty

日
本
の
生
き
方

Ikigai

The Japanese are communal animals, not just social animals. People identify themselves very strongly in groups, whether that is in their workplaces, their families, alumni groups, teams they support, hobbies, and so on.

In Western stories, plots usually follow protagonists asserting their individuality against society – Billy Elliot finding his calling in dance despite the opposition of his family, or Rocky discovering the winner in himself despite the losers in his community. In Japan, typical stories go the other way. The Seven Samurai become a force through teamwork, while in *Spirited Away*, the main character starts the story as an indifferent girl, but develops into the lead role by insisting that she be allowed to work in the weird bathhouse of the fantasy world in which she finds herself.

This might have its roots in Japan's long agricultural tradition. It took a village to grow rice. Irrigation required village-wide compromise among community members as to the source and use of water. Planting and harvesting rice demanded village-wide cooperation. To be an outcast meant guaranteed starvation. The Japanese have a word for it: *murahachibu* (村八分). It literally means to divide a village into 80 percent. If someone is *murahachibu*, it means that the person has been ostracised by the majority of the community to which he or she used to belong.

Such allegiance to, and dependence on, a community used to be seen as one of the cultural traits that hindered the development of Japan into a more Western liberal society. It is true that the still-strong tradition of life-long employment has contributed to the rigid labour market in Japan, and continues to hinder the Japanese economy from realising its more dynamic potential. Nevertheless, there is no denying that acceptance into a community and recognition of one's contribution to it forms an important part of any individual's sense of his or her own worth. Even if that is only a part of a person's purpose in life, it gives that person a deep sense of satisfaction.

The Japanese call that satisfaction *ikigai* (生きがい): realising the value of one's life. The word is a combination of two separate words. *Iki* (生き) means 'life' or 'living', while *kai* (甲斐) means 'effect' or 'result'. A close translation in English would actually be a French phrase: *raison d'être*.

In a world of free agents living inside the comfort of their own bubbles, an increased sense of belonging and a search for *ikigai* may do more than a little good for the mindset of the global community.

Culture, Art
and Style

Modern literature

The birth of popular literature began towards the end of the Edo period. Hundreds of publishing houses competed for readers by engaging popular writers to create love stories, historical novels, comic stories, and so on. They all catered to popular tastes. However, with the Meiji Reformation in the mid-19th century, literature became somewhat highbrow. This arguably started with Natsume Sōseki (夏目漱石 1867–1916). Sōseki was a man who suffered with mental health problems, and who studied in England for about two years at the turn of the 20th century to study British literature and learn English teaching methods.

On his return to Japan, and by way of helping his anxiety issues, he started to write stories about his cat. The story, *Wagahai wa neko de aru* (吾輩は猫である – *I Am a Cat*), was serialised in a respected *haiku* magazine and became an instant hit. This new style of literature created by intellectuals like Sōseki created the division between *junbugaku* (純文学 – 'pure literature') and *taishū bungaku* (大衆文学 – 'popular literature').

There are many reasons for this, but a major factor was the change in Japanese writing style. Previously, written Japanese was different from the spoken version of the language. Around the time of the Meiji Reformation, Japanese writers started to write Japanese as it was spoken, in a style called *genbun'itchi* (言文一致). Progressive writers like Sōseki were well-educated and wrote in this modern style. Writers of popular literature were creatures of habit, and took some time to adopt this new trend. It created a strange situation where more highbrow literature, with less humour, was modern, while popular literature was more traditional.

Even now, the distinction survives. Bungeishunjū (文藝春秋), a major publishing house, gives out two of the most prestigious literature prizes twice a year. One is the Akutagawa Prize (芥川賞), given to the best newcomer in pure literature, and named after the author Ryūnosuke Akutagawa (芥川龍之介 1892–1927). The other is the Naoki Prize (直木賞), given to the best work of popular literature and named after Sanjūgo Naoki (直木三十五 1891–1934).

The prizes do much to promote literature in Japan, but categorisation is restricting budding authors. Those aiming for pure literature are becoming more introspective, sometimes to the point of claustrophobia. At the same time, literature with some entertainment value is regarded as less valid than the highbrow, self-obsessed opuses.

Ambitious storytellers seem to be finding more freedom in outlets such as animation and the new trend of *lanobe* (ラノベ), or 'light novels'. These dispense with the shackles of intellectual expectations of 'literature' by self-appointed arbiters of taste.

The Japanese love to read, and their writers are happy to cater for that insatiable appetite for good stories. It is just that the literary establishment seems to be woefully out of touch with the changing world and its readership.

Words with no direct translation

Most Japanese words and expressions that can't easily be translated into English share some common traits: they are generally expressions which recognise and reinforce the communal ties that bind people, or they relate to a typically Japanese philosophy.

For example...

いただきます You say **itadakimasu** before you start a meal, just as you might say *bon appétit* in French, but it is a word of thanks for what you're about to eat. The literal translation is 'Allow me to have this for myself', which expresses modesty as well as gratitude. The gratitude directed not only towards the host and cook, but also the farmers, fishermen, and even natural phenomena such as sunshine and rainfall, that all contributed to the creation of the meal.

ごちそうさまでした At the end of a meal, say **gochisōsama-deshita**. The word *chisō* (馳走) originally referred to the task of acquiring all the ingredients necessary for a feast, so the literal translation is something akin to, 'What a *chisō* it must have been!'. In other words, 'Thank you so much for making the necessary effort to prepare such a splendid meal'. It is an expression of gratitude directed at the host and cook.

おつかれさま **Otsukaresama** is an acknowledgement of someone's hard work. The direct translation is 'You must be tired' – but the tiredness does not have a negative connotation. Rather, it is the natural state for someone who has laboured long and hard for the benefit of a task. You are giving that person recognition for their contribution.

おすそわけ **Osusowake** means 'sharing the hem' – but makes no sense in the context of western clothes. The hems of a kimono are always divided left and right, until you close the front and tie it at the waist with an *obi* belt. Some linguistic acrobatics are required here, but *osusowake* means that you share a gift with someone else, just as the hem of a kimono always flows away to the left and right. If you receive a box full of apples from a family member who is a farmer, you would share some of them with your neighbour, saying 'This is *osusowake*', giving it the nuance that this is not a special gift, but the mere sharing of our good fortune, as naturally as the hem of a kimono flows both ways.

日本の生き方

おかげさま A translation of **okagesama** is 'Thanks to you', but the Japanese use this expression for almost everything. If someone recognises that you have recovered from a common cold, you could reply *'Okagesama', or,* 'Thanks to you, I have recovered' – even if that person hasn't had anything to do with your cold at all. What you are recognising is not a specific causation or contribution made by the addressee, but the connection that both of you have by belonging to the same community. It is similar to the English poet John Donne's principle of 'No man is an island'.

つまらないものですが Say **'tsumaranai mono desuga'** when you are giving a gift. Paradoxically, it means 'This is such an uninteresting thing'. The Japanese, not wishing to make a recipient feel obliged, downplay the value of a gift. It is the show of modesty that lubricates social interactions.

お邪魔します **Ojama shimasu** is similar in spirit to *tsumaranai mono desuga* and is used when you are invited to someone's home. Literally, it means 'I will be a disturbance to you'. Of course, this is not a declaration of one's intention to raise hell in somebody else's abode – it is simply a show of modesty by way of giving thanks for the invitation and to reassure the host that you will be careful not to cause unnecessary inconveniences.

おたがいさま The direct translation of **otagaisama** would be 'As you are, I am', or 'As you do, I do'. If someone apologises to you for being late, you say *'otagaisama'* to convey the sentiment of 'not to worry, it could have easily been me who was late'.

寂しい **Sabishii** refers to a typical Japanese philosophy. Sabi is the same word used in Wabi-Sabi, and is an aesthetic philosophy that refers to a state of incompleteness. This incompleteness may refer to the absence of a person, as in 'I miss you', or simply a general state of resignation as to the imperfect nature of the world around us.

仕方ない The nearest translation of **Shikata-nai** is 'It cannot be helped'. Shikata means a way, method or means and Nai denotes the absence thereof, so together they translate as 'There is no way'. This may sound negative to an unaccustomed ear, but it is an expression of resigned acceptance of what has come to pass. This philosophy helps renewal and regrowth in a country where natural geography and climate can result in sudden violent earthquakes, typhoons and volcanic eruptions. In this way, the expression has a certain therapeutic value for people, when faced with uncertainty.

日本の生き方

風情 **Fuzei** describes an aesthetic appeal that can be applied to scenery, artistry and people. This is different from mere 'beauty'. The closest English term would probably be 'style', but this Japanese word is often used to describe a state that is not obviously pleasing. A ragged coastline in stormy weather, the early morning mist rising silently in a forest, well-used tea cups, or even an old lady's wrinkled hands can all be described as Fuzei-no-aru, or 'full of Fuzei'. This is a compliment borne out of a very Japanese philosophy of value beyond sheer beauty.

粋 or 意気 **Iki** was traditionally a word associated with the common people of Edo (Tokyo) during the Edo Period, particularly in the 18th and 19th century. It is a word used to describe city residents or urban folk, who typically have a lively, although not necessarily extravagant, lifestyle. The term is also associated with tidiness and cleanliness.

The Tale of Genji

Genji Monogatari (源氏物語), or *The Tale of Genji*, is believed to be the oldest novel in the world. Written by Murasaki Shikibu (紫式部), a lady-in-waiting who lived in the late 10th and early 11th century, it tells the story of the life and loves (lots of loves) of the eponymous Hikaru Genji, the son of an emperor.

To develop a national literature was not a smooth process for Japan, a country and culture without its own writing system. It is also telling that a woman was the first notable writer of fiction.

Before we developed our phonetic alphabet known as *kana*, the Japanese used Chinese characters for the written word, based on their phonetic value. Official records were kept in straight Chinese, albeit in a bastardised form. There are usually many strokes in any single Chinese character, which represents a meaning. Using any of them for a single phonetic value makes terrible economic sense.

There are two types of *kana*: *katakana* (片仮名) and *hiragana* (平仮名). They were developed by either using a part of each Chinese character (*katakana*), or using a simplified writing system of each Chinese character (*hiragana*). *Katakana* was mostly used to make Chinese texts easier to read for the Japanese. *Hiragana*, unusually, was used by women.

Government life, which was almost exclusively male, was filled with the Chinese language and its writing system. Men generally thought writing Japanese using *kana* was effeminate and beneath them. Of course, having recourse only to a foreign language and a limited ability to express themselves in it, men had few literary outlets. They could write poetry, which was the exclusive domain of Japanese language and open to both sexes, but men were also expected to be able to write poetry in Chinese in the manner of classical poets from China such as Li Bai (李白) or Du Fu (杜甫). Those attempts must have been poor, as very little of those works remain.

The Tale of Genji tells the story of the aforementioned emperor's son who loses his mother at a young age, and falls in love with one of his father's concubines. Laden with a sense of unfulfilled love (and serious mother issues), Hikaru Genji sets out on a life filled with romantic conquests and broken hearts. The whole saga centres around the male princely protagonist, but one wonders if he really is the main theme of the story. For one thing, his character hardly develops until, towards the end of the tale, he holds his baby in his hands, all the while knowing that the baby's real father is one of his protégés – he then experiences an epiphany of karmic irony. On the other hand the reader is left with vivid images of many female characters who come into, and invariably leave, Genji's life. It seems that Murasaki Shikibu wanted to write a story *not* of a Don Juan-like prince, but about the reality of court life from a female perspective. She did so in Japanese and using the *hiragana* reserved for women. While men went about their rigid and ostentatious lives, clumsy in their language and emotions, Murasaki kept it real and became a national treasure.

行く春や
鳥啼き魚の
目は泪

Spring is passing.
The birds cry, and the fishes fill
With tears in their eyes.

Bashō, 1689

Haiku

In the literary parlour game *renga* (連歌), or 'chain of songs', the 5-7-5-7-7 syllable structure of *waka* is divided into two. The first person composes the 5-7-5 part, and the second person completes the poem by adding their own 7-7. The next person then plays on this first collaborative piece by adding another 5-7-5, developing the theme proposed in the first set, and another person adds 7-7 lines. This goes on among the participants for a predetermined number of times, usually 100.

During the Heian period, people held *renga* parties where the host and guests brought their individual literary tastes and education into creating this collaborative art and contest of *bons mots*. Usually, there was a noted poet of the time in attendance to give advice and suggest amendments. They were called *renga-shi* (連歌師), or masters of the form.

Renga contributed greatly to the development of Japanese literary culture and it spread among the populace. It continued to be popular well into the Edo period, but in the 17th century another trend occurred in which only the first 5-7-5, or *hokku* (発句), began to stand on its own as a composition. This was the birth of *haiku* (俳句).

As poetry became popularised through its various forms and context, there was a tendency of the tone of composition to become less arty and more, for the lack of a better word, vulgar. For an English speaker, it would have been as if people had stopped aspiring to Shakespeare's sonnets and settled for concocting funny limericks instead. Witticism and clever punchlines were valued over artistic sensibilities.

The comedic *haiku*, called *senryū* (川柳), remains popular today, but was limiting the potential of new shorter forms of poetry. The poet who changed this slide was Matsuo Bashō (松尾芭蕉1644–1694). He gained fame and fans through witty compositions, very much in keeping with the fashion of the time. Nevertheless, he dispensed with the popularity and pursued the *haiku* compositions which reflected his own artistic sensibilities and personal feelings. Luckily for him, his movement gathered strength during his lifetime.

Haiku continues to be popular in modern Japan. All major newspapers in Japan invite readers to submit their compositions on a regular basis, and professional *haiku* masters select and publish the ones they like.

The popularity is based on two things. One is simplicity – the 5-7-5 structure is accessible to all, and does not require long and arduous mental labour for composition. The second is the freedom of its subject matter – Bashō's movement allowed people's ordinary feelings to be expressed in poetic style. It can be funny and witty, or sombre and intelligent. Everyday thoughts and observations are fit for poetic treatment, to be appreciated by a sympathetic audience. It has become a true popular art.

Waka: poetry as a social skill

Somehow, ancient Japanese people decided their language sounded better – more rhythmical and meaningful – when uttered in groups of five and seven syllables. It was the birth of Japanese poetry, or *waka* (和歌).

The structure of these poems differed wildly in the early days. Some were longer, line after line of five- and seven-syllable combinations, but later the 5-7-5-7-7 structure emerged as standard.

In the courtly life of the Heian period (8th–12th century), writing *waka* became an important social skill, especially in relation to matters of the heart. Both men and women were judged for their character and intelligence on their ability to compose these poems. In *The Tale of Genji*, one sees this in practice. Court ladies led secluded lives deep in their residences, surrounded by their ladies-in-waiting. Suitors only caught glimpses of them, and assumed their physical beauty by reputation. To initiate courtship, a man had to send a well-crafted poem declaring his desire to be more intimately acquainted with the lady. The lady favoured the man with a reply also in the form of poetry. To indicate 'I am not that into you', the reply might have been written by one of her ladies-in-waiting, reminding the suitor of the inappropriateness of the match. If the initial poem was well written and the author was of good repute based on the information gathered by her ladies-in-waiting, the lady herself might have composed a reply and, better still, written it herself on suitably stylish stationery. It was important that these poems were witty and showed the author's intelligence and education. For this purpose, lesser men and women of letters had to collect noted poets among their staff or ladies-in-waiting to act as ghostwriters and literary advisers. Famous female literary figures of this period, including Murasaki Shikibu, the author of *The Tale of Genji*, were usually one of those retainers surrounding aristocratic ladies.

With his passion now whipped into a frenzy by the lady's handwriting (which could also have belonged to someone with better penmanship), the suitor would make a daring nocturnal visit to the lady. If the match was deemed appropriate, the gates would open and the lovers would spend a night of passion together under insufficient lighting or by moonlight.

It was regarded as bad form for the man to stay late into the morning – he was expected to beat a retreat in the morning mist. Still, the most important task remained. The man had to compose yet another suitably tender poem to his lady. It was called *kinuginu no uta* (後朝の歌), literally a 'morning-after poem'. It was basically a thank-you note to praise the lady's beauty and express the sorrow of parting. It was important for this to reach the lady promptly, as any tardiness suggested disappointment on the man's part. There is a tale of a man who neglected to send the morning-after poem, having been smothered by his official business during the day after the tryst, which resulted in his distraught lover becoming a nun. Had Shakespeare's Ophelia been Japanese, she would not have wasted her time picking flowers.

日
本
の
生
き
方

If the courtship went well and the lovers became a steady couple, they announced their partnership publicly with a ceremony called *tokoro arawashi* (床顕し), literally meaning 'exposing the bed'. They were then regarded as husband and wife by society. This was the form of marriage amongst Heian aristocrats. The wife would remain with her family, and any children resulting from the match were raised with her family as well.

There were 21 anthologies of waka poems assembled at the emperor's command between the 10th and 15th centuries, each representing the style, taste and fashion of poetry at the time.

秋山に落つる黄葉しましくは
な散り乱ひそ
妹があたり見む

On this autumn mountain
Tumbling yellowed leaves
For just a moment
Cease your scattering
For I would see my beloved's home.

Author unknown, c. AD 759

Kabuki theatre

The social upheaval created by the Age of Warring States (between the 15th and 17th centuries, not to be confused with a similarly named much earlier period in China) gave people room to express their individuality. When the era drew to a close and peace returned, commerce flourished and people were hungry for entertainment. Kyoto regained its status as Japan's capital, and entertainers gathered on the riverside of the nearby Kamo River, which was regarded as being outside the city's jurisdiction. One

of the more famous performers was a female dancer and impresario called Izumo no Okuni (出雲阿国 born c.1572), who gained fame by staging what she called *kabuki odori* or '*kabuki* dance'. The word *kabuki* (歌舞伎) is derived from the verb *kabuku*, meaning 'to lean' or 'to be out of the ordinary'. Kabuki in this context was used to denote a show's outrageousness – it is said that performances were very erotic in tone. Before long, female performers were banned by the authorities. However, the show went on, as they say.

As civil life continued to thrive, the urban population demanded popular entertainment. The traditional performing art of *Noh* theatre was for samurai, and it had (and continues to have) many structural limitations. Nevertheless, it did provide a springboard for the popular theatre that emerged in this period.

From the start, the essence of *kabuki* has been its popular appeal. Actors don outrageous costumes and wear eye-catching make-up. The more extravagant the stage sets, the better the audience's appreciation. Performances can be divided into two categories: one, which mainly features dance, and the other featuring straight drama. Dramas can be further divided into historical plays (though hardly accurate) and those that take their themes from contemporary life.

Kabuki continues to be popular in Japan today, and many *kabuki* actors work in film and TV. However, one of the unfortunate features of *kabuki* theatre is its hereditary system. There are a number of *kabuki* actor families, and famous actors' names are usually passed on from father to son. Therefore, we have Ichikawa Ebizō XI, Nakamura Kanzaburō XVIII, and Onoe Kikugorō VII, for example. Name succession is a big event in *kabuki* theatre, and fans debate endlessly whether or not a young star is ready to fill his predecessor's shoes. It maintains prestige and is a nice

日
本
の
生
き
方

gimmick for promoters. Still, the sense of tradition can prevent fresh talents from shining, and is terribly anachronistic.

Having said that, a visit to a *kabuki* theatre is a treat. *Kabuki-za* (歌舞伎座), a theatre in the Ginza district of Tokyo, has been recently renovated to a fine standard. They also have a fantastic earphone-based guide in English, which explains the performance as it is played on stage. You don't have to stay for the whole performance, and can go in for just one act. I heartily recommend a visit to bask in the glory of this 'anything goes' show-business world.

Noh theatre

Noh (能) is a difficult performing art to get into. First of all, there is the issue of terminology and history. The name usually refers to the type of performing art where the actors perform certain roles on stage, accompanied by musical performers. These were collectively called *sarugaku* (猿楽) until the Meiji Reformation. Faced with the threat of extinction caused by a developing Japanese society and the decline of the traditional audience of samurai, the Meiji government resurrected this tradition artificially, calling the art form *nohgaku* (能楽).

Secondly, this artificial resuscitation resulted in the art form falling between two stools: one of a strict traditionalist dogma, and another of the need to acquiesce to the demands of modern audiences. While the performance, which used to take a whole day, has been shortened to about two hours today, the repertoire has remained limited, sticking to tradition at the expense of popular appeal.

In any event, *Noh* represents the origin of the Japanese performing arts scene, and it would be remiss not to touch upon it here. *Noh* plays always have two principal actors, called *shite* (シテ) and *waki* (ワキ). A *shite* is the main character, usually a god or a ghost. Prompted by the *waki* actor, the *shite* actor recounts certain past events, almost always tragic, through song and dance. The audience is thereby invited to share in the ghostly supernatural experience unfolding on the stage.

The *Noh* performance is followed by *kyōgen* (狂言), which are comedic sketches depicting comic moments from daily life, giving contrast to the preceding haunting experience. The best-known *kyōgen* plays involve a comedy of errors acted out by a dim master and his equally dim servant.

In recent years, some *kyōgen* actors, such as Mansai Nomura (野村萬斎), have broken the barrier and become successful film actors. *Kyōgen*, with its comedic appeal, is relatively easier for a modern audience to appreciate. However, *Noh* remains a truly acquired taste. It is undoubtedly a valuable cultural heritage, resonating with Greek tragedies and associated arts. Its costumes, masks, music, poetry and dance formed the basis from which various other crafts and performing arts have sprung.

日本の生き方

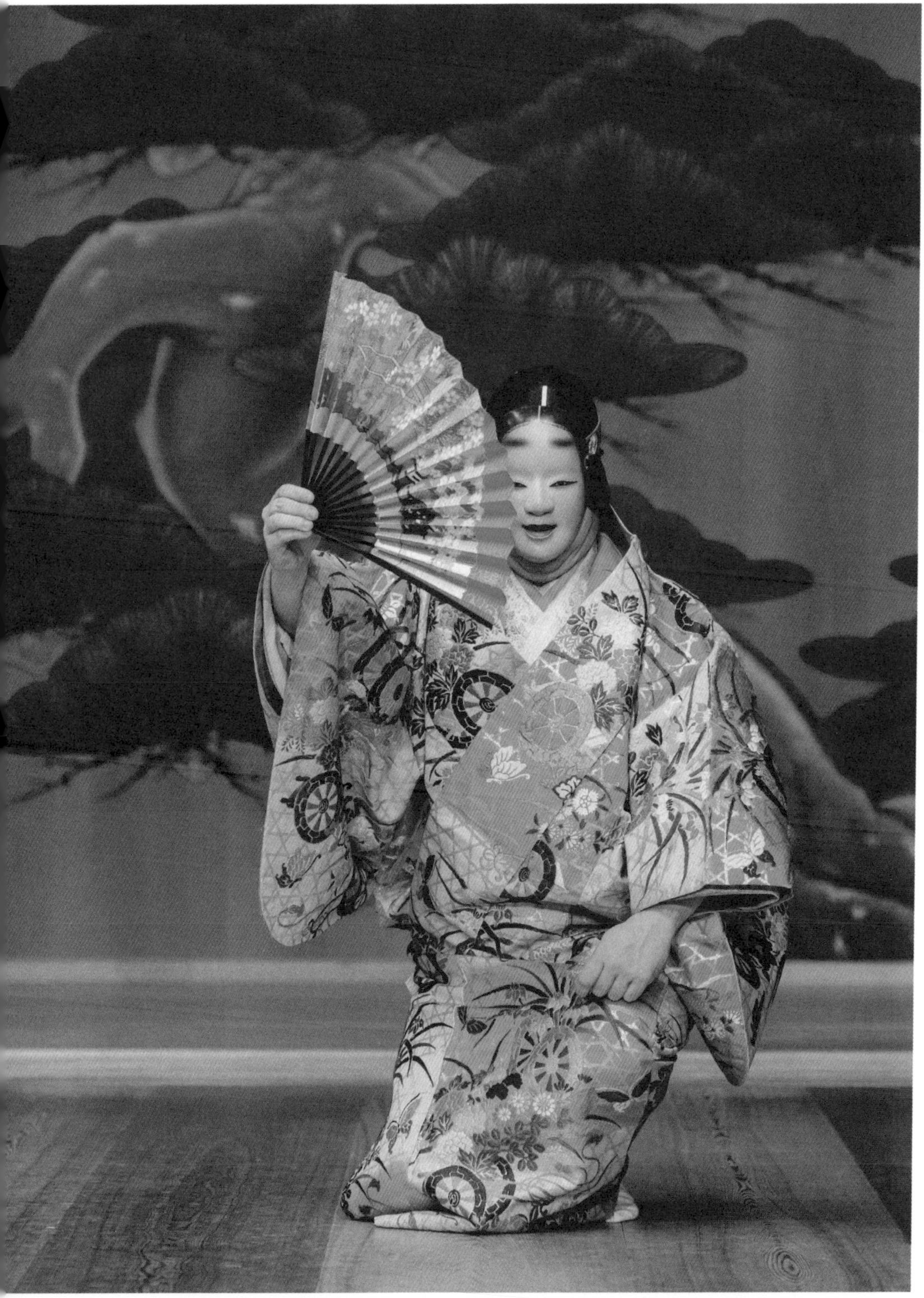

Architecture: from shrines and temples to castles

Despite the land being prone to devastating natural disasters, Japan boasts many well-preserved historical buildings. Such buildings often represent powers-that-have-been. In the Confucian-influenced Chinese tradition of *Tian Ming*, or the 'Mandate of Heaven', any representations of past power, especially buildings, were likely to be destroyed by a new emergent power by way of a celebratory bonfire for the refreshed 'mandate'. The Japanese have always been more frugal, maintaining and reusing old buildings, seeing spiritual significance in structures which have survived through the thick and thin of historical upheaval.

Thanks to this tendency to preserve old buildings, historic buildings in Japan look a lot more ancient than their Chinese or Korean equivalents, even though Japanese history is much younger. From city planning to palace buildings and temple towers, both Korea and Japan followed the Chinese example. For a Japanese national style to emerge, the Chinese style had to be adapted to suit Japan's climate and lifestyle. This primarily meant building for the sit-on-the-floor style of living. The Japanese did not take to chairs until recently and this meant that Japanese houses tended to be built with lower ceilings and roofs. As for climate, the Chinese closed-wall style did not suit the high temperature and humidity of Japanese summers. Kenkō (兼好 1284–1350), was a Buddhist monk who wrote essays collected together as *Tsurezuregusa* (徒然草 – *Essays in Idleness*). In one of them, Kenkō explains that, 'A house should be built with summer in mind.'. As a result, traditional Japanese houses tend to be more open, with wide windows and doors to the outside world. Another common feature is a raised floor, which prevents humidity from seeping through from the earth to the building. This style is exemplified in Shōsō-in (正倉院), a treasure house in Nara prefecture, but is common among traditional houses.

Another original Japanese invention was the castle. During the Age of Warring States, warlords built castles to protect their territories. At first, they were more like forts than proper castles, built on mountains or hilltops for better protection and with no ornament. Later, as the warlords' grasp on economic activities became more crucial, castles were built on the plain, at the crossroads of commercial routes, or in places with easy access to ports and internal waterways. To maintain the defensive strength of such buildings, they adopted stonewalls, moats, tiled roofs, earthen walls, elaborate defensive plans and labyrinthine designs. To top it all off, warlords started building towers, or donjons, called *tenshukaku* (天守閣), as the centrepiece of castles. Such towers had little defensive purpose – in fact, a tall structure with hollow internal space burned all too easily when attacked. Nevertheless, the structure, with its elaborate design combining roofs, eaves and gables to make it look even taller, demonstrated and symbolised the power and authority of the warlords and became an essential part

日本の生き方

of the Japanese architectural scenery. One example is the well-preserved Himejijō (姫路城), a castle in Hyōgo prefecture.

Contrary to the tender love and care the Japanese have given to their ancient buildings, Japan's modern constructions are scrap-and-build affairs. Inspired by the rapid capital depreciation rate of buildings as fixed assets, and the accounting wizardry based on it, landlords tend to build for a quick cash return rather than creating something that will last. As a result, Japan boasts an inordinate number of qualified architects (around 500,000 are registered), but not much in the way of characterful city scenery.

With the extreme urbanisation of the population that has occurred in the last century or so, and the easing of building height restrictions (putting trust in technological advancements to counter the threat of earthquakes), cities are growing upwards, as well as becoming more energy efficient. It will, I think, take several decades more for the definitive modern Japanese style of architecture to emerge.

Celebrity culture

In Japan, regular television broadcasts started in 1953, and TV sets became very popular in Japanese households around the time of the Tokyo Olympics in 1964. TV continues to play a big part in Japanese life today.

Prior to the dominance of TV, celebrities came from the film industry. However, while actors commanded the adoration of fans, their exposure was limited. With the advent of TV, they were able to appear on peoples' screens each week, or in some cases, every day. The demand for TV personalities – actors, comedians or mere presenters – became huge. To make matters even more desperate, Tokyo had seven TV stations by the mid-60s, each competing for the attention of insatiable viewers.

The demand was met by agencies who managed such personalities, called *talento* in Japanese English. The number of such instant *talento* celebrities increased in direct inverse correlation to the actual talent possessed by those going before the cameras.

In the 80s, stressed-out TV executives happened upon a brilliant idea. They realised that those appearing on TV did not have to be special in any way. Amateur singers, slapstick comedians, and

other entertainment talents (to use all those words in the loosest possible way) flooded the airwaves. The TV camera was turned on to the viewers. Japan was decades ahead of the reality show trend in the West.

In the past, record deals used to be nice little earners for Japanese film stars, providing them with an extra income on the side. That said, in the past those who could not sing did not try.

More recently, with a plethora of TV celebrities scraping the bottom of the ever-decreasing money pot of the entertainment industry, the market was flooded with manufactured and autotuned music known as *J-pop*. If a single voice cannot hold an audience (let alone a tune), they are packaged together as various boy and girl groups in true cheaper-by-the-dozen fashion. One of the most extreme examples is, AKB48, a girl group which has more than 100 members (the 48 refers to the original number of members in 2005).

After decades of this business model, the quality of entertainment on Japanese TV is beyond low. Dramas are either reruns, remakes or copies of past hits. Even news programmes have long been dumbed down, as exemplified by continuous attempts to turn female anchors into objectified pop-culture celebrities in the most hideous show of Japanese misogyny.

Not surprisingly, despite the statistically proven huge number of hours spent in front of the TV, the Japanese have finally begun to desert it, especially the young ones. Apart from the national public broadcaster, NHK, all other major TV stations are privately owned and subsidiaries of newspaper companies. As ratings decline, so does advertisement revenue, resulting in even direr production quality. At the same time, those *talento* agencies are coming under scrutiny due to exploitative contracts and harsh business practices.

Still, TV stations are using their lobbying powers with politicians, who cannot stoop low enough to get positive televisual exposure, to stifle competition. As a result, Japan has not seen any new competitors entering the TV business since the 60s.

In any event, the current status quo cannot be maintained for long. It is a veritable clattering train with no one in charge.

Kimono

Kimonos were everyday wear well into the Meiji period (1868–1912) and Taishō period (1912–1926). Western-style clothes, such as suits for men and dresses for women, were reserved for office work and special occasions. However, these Western styles became increasingly popular, especially after the introduction of casual clothes following the Second World War, and the roles reversed. Gradually, kimonos came to be worn only for special occasions, such as New Year's Day celebrations, for Coming of Age Day in mid-January by people who have reached the age of 20, weddings, and so on. As a result, kimonos became ornate and very expensive, to be fit for the special occasions for which they were to be worn. The casual kimono nearly disappeared from the marketplace.

This trend reversed in the 1990s. It started with yukata (浴衣), casual kimonos for the summer season which became fashionable among young women. Yukatas are cheaper than a full kimono set, and are a nice way to stand out. Following this initial spark, there was a boom for recycled kimonos in the 2000s.

The Western-style clothes market is saturated with brand names in an industry that promotes changing trends each season. This must induce status anxiety. Consumers end up paying too much for the clothes, only to look like everybody else in accordance with the fashion diktat of the day. Kimonos are a good way out of this uniformity.

Being out of fashion for some time, there are few rules about the way one is supposed to wear a kimono. One is allowed freedom of expression in choosing their style – there are even kimonos made of denim.

Personally, I like the kimono because I feel it is designed to make ordinary people look good. They are loose-fitting and do not presume that everybody has a narrow waist in the way designer-label clothes do. And they look way better than a T-shirt-and-stretch-pants combo. One drawback may be that kimonos do not do winter very well.

Harajuku girls

Tokyo developed from east to west. To the west of the city spread the pastoral lands owned mostly by temples and shrines, where tenant farmers grew vegetables for the ever-increasing city dwellers. As the city was developing, Harajuku (原宿) was an inn town (宿) in that countryside.

Following the Meiji Reformation of the mid-19th century, the area to the north of Harajuku (present-day Yoyogi Park [代々木公園]), became the training ground for the army. After the Second World War, the same area was appropriated by the Americans for their military barracks. For the first time in its history, this brought to the area some semblance of 'cutting edge', with the presence of 'exotic foreigners'.

In 1964, the Olympic Games were held in Tokyo, and the now formerly American area was turned into Yoyogi National Gymnasium, as well as the athletes' village. Harajuku had come under the spotlight as a smart area with an air of modernity and international sophistication, with the nearby 'park life' in Yoyogi Park, a concept which was alien to most Japanese at that stage. In the 1970s, with post-war economic growth flourishing into a blustering consumer culture, a commercial complex was built that housed many boutique fashion labels, designer shops, Harajuku was put firmly on track to become the fashion hub that it is today.

Shops, cafés and art spaces continued to pop up in the area. In the 1980s, the local council closed certain streets to traffic in the area and made them pedestrian-only at weekends. This attracted buskers and group dancers, with one well-known tribe known as *takenoko-zoku* (竹の子族), meaning 'Bamboo-shoot people' (don't ask me why). They dressed outrageously, but somehow danced in unison, in a true Japanese tribute to homogeneity. The area attracted more than 100,000 people a day at its height and these crowds led the authorities to cease the pedestrian-only days in 1998. The musicians, dancers and other event-goers moved to Yoyogi Park and its surrounding areas.

Harajuku continues to attract fashion-industry types, and it is the place to gauge trends, launch new concepts and test new brands. Its reputation as the cutting edge of Japanese fashion attracts tourists from all over the world, creating a global vibe. You can see edgily dressed young women going window shopping on any given day in Harajuku, although these days you cannot automatically assume they are all Japanese. That's just another snapshot of the place, which has gone through many reinventions of itself in its short history.

日本の生き方

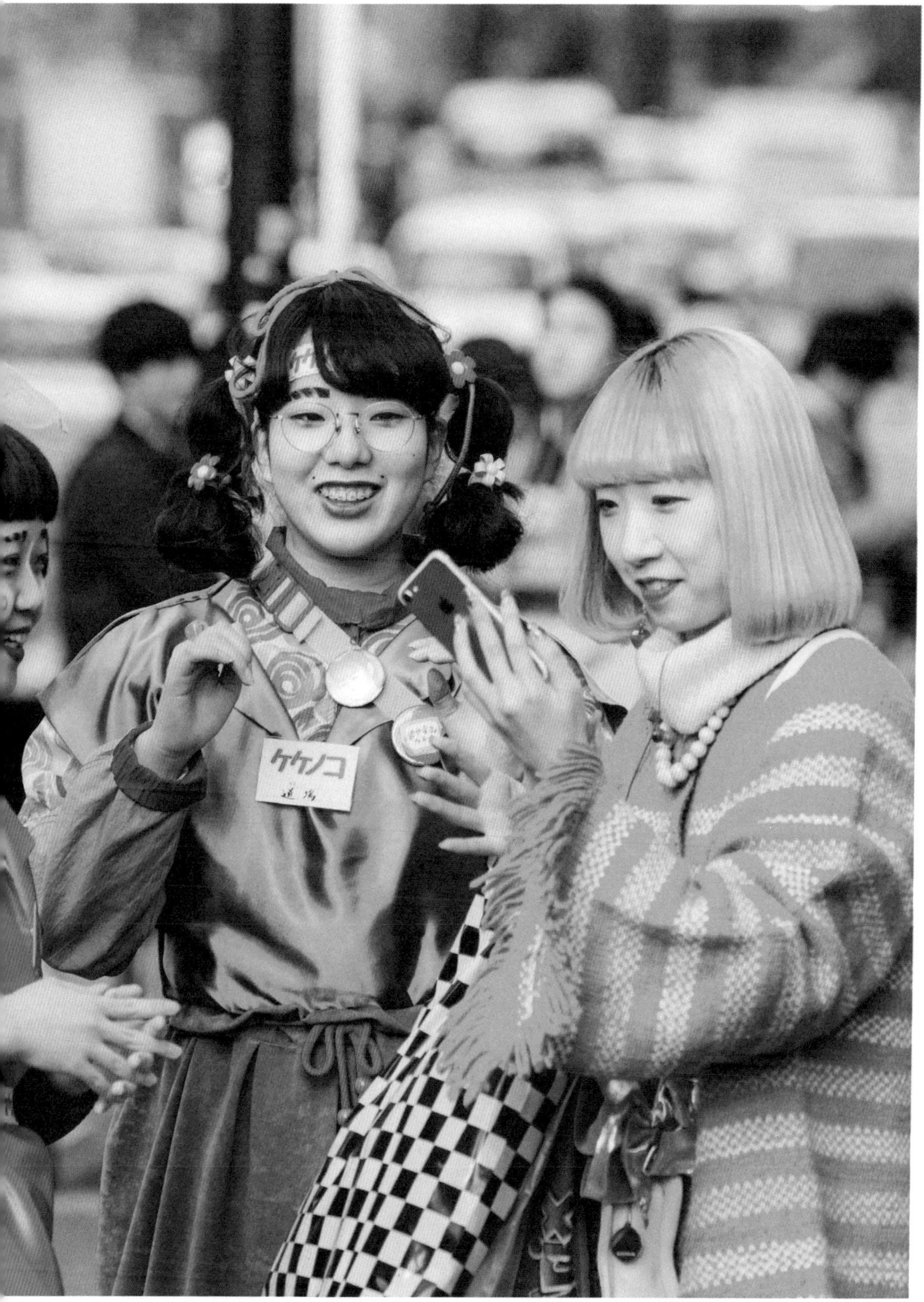
ケケノコ

Cool Biz and Warm Biz

In 2005, the Japanese government launched a campaign called *Cool Biz* to encourage people to dispense with ties and jackets in the workplace during the summer season. The purpose was to cut energy consumption by lessening the need for using air-con during the summer months.

The campaign was a roaring success. People, especially men, were freed from the social norm of having to have tight collars and wear clothes made of wool during hot and humid Japanese summers. The lower energy use resulted in the reduction of about 1.14 million tons of CO2 per summer, according to government statistics.

The campaign also benefited the clothing industry, as people tried to find a new fashion standard for the office. Bright dress shirts became popular, some featuring coloured stitches and buttons.

Following the reduced use of nuclear power after the disaster at Fukushima, the government launched the *Super Cool Biz* campaign in 2012, suggesting that men could now wear polo shirts and even Hawaiian shirts in the workplace. This seems to have had less success than its predecessor – even the more adventurous Japanese businessman seems to have found it difficult to go *that* colourful.

Not as well known as *Cool Biz*, is its sister campaign, *Warm Biz*, which was launched at the same time. As its name suggests, *Warm Biz* aimed to lessen energy consumption by encouraging people to wear more layers to decrease reliance on heaters during winter. It was perhaps lesser known than *Cool Biz* because people generally do not need government encouragement to put on a jumper.

Seven years after its initial launch, *Cool Biz* seems to have been firmly accepted by the Japanese people. In a way, it has hit the sweetest of sweet spots in environmental policy-making: it was something everybody could do, and everybody *wanted* to do. Plus, it was good for the environment.

Ninja

The history of ninja goes back a long way. The word literally means 'spy', and the history of spying and the use of clandestine means to achieve victory in wars is as old as the history of warfare itself. Sun Tzu, the great Chinese strategic thinker, famously said, 'Know your enemy and know yourself'. The value of intelligence and the means to acquire it have never gone out of fashion.

For spies to flourish, there has to be a state of war or at least the threat of it. The Age of Warring States in Japan provided an ideal background. Samurai warlords divided the country into their separate fiefdoms and vied for survival. If they were lucky, they achieved supremacy over their neighbours in a hostile environment.

However, the culture and traditions of the samurai did not suit the clandestine work demanded of spies. Each samurai clan was guaranteed the safety of their person and property in return for their allegiance to the warlord. Battles were important opportunities for samurai to prove their allegiance and to gain reward for their valour. For this purpose, their actions in battle had to be conspicuous and recognised. Samurai of earlier times used to make a speech before going to fight, ensuring that not only enemies, but comrades knew of their presence and the deeds which were about to be committed. Even when mass infantry fighting became the norm, samurai warriors found a way to get noticed, decorating their armour extravagantly so everybody was aware of their presence. In short, samurai made poor ninja.

Because of this, warlords had to rely on people outside the samurai class for clandestine work. In the lulls between wars, the task usually fell to monks and performing artists. What these groups had in common was freedom of movement. While commoners were tied to their lands, monks and performers could cross the boundaries of the warlords' spheres of influence relatively easily. They could also rely on the hospitality of warlords in return for the intelligence they carried.

In times of battle, warlords could not avail themselves of monks or performers conveniently travelling around the battlefields. To gather information and carry out clandestine missions such as depriving a besieged fort of its water supply or starting a fire in the midst of an enemy encampment, warlords had to rely on low-class samurai. High-class samurai could not be asked to carry out such demeaning tasks – the volunteer had to be desperate enough to agree to such a mission.

Constant warfare sustained the demand for such specialists, and two regions became known for supplying more skilled professionals than any other. One was Kōga (甲賀), in present-day Shiga Prefecture (滋賀県). The other was Iga (伊賀), in present-day Mie Prefecture (三重). They were both relatively close to Kyoto to get the latest news, and their lands were mountainous. The geography worked both ways, though. While it protected them from any direct rule by a powerful overlord, their crop yields were limited. Under the circumstances, their skilled labour in espionage was what they ended up trading to the highest bidder in the time of civil wars.

日本の生き方

The actual effect that ninja had on Japanese history is not well known. Much of the detail about them was created in storybooks that became popular during the later peacetime of the Edo period and beyond. The ninja's black costume, straight *katana* sword, and *shuriken* flying star weapons were all fictional inventions.

The appeal of the ninja is that they were little people with extraordinary skills, fighting against the harshness of life and the tide of time. In typical tales, they fight against the inevitable coming of the authoritarian Tokugawa shogunate. Through such stories, ninja realise everyday fantasies in fictional settings.

Land of artisans

The Japanese industrial revolution was achieved almost as if it were on steroids. As the Meiji Reformation government opened up Japan to Western civilisation in the mid-19th century, Western-style factories and industrial plants were introduced to Japan *en masse* and in a relatively short period of time.

This, of course, was a shock to Japan's artisanal manufacturers. However, those who had withstood the initial onslaught of industrialisation did have a chance to survive long after the impact.

In traditional crafts such as pottery, woodwork, lacquering, weaving, swordsmithing, and carpentry, the Japanese had – and still have – a long tradition of skilled craftsmanship which had been handed down through family lines or from masters to apprentices.

The Japanese aesthetic, in the long tradition of the values of *wabi-sabi* (finding beauty in imperfections), which were nurtured in the culture of the tea ceremony, also supported the survival of such craftsmanship. Industrially manufactured goods might have represented economic progression, but the beauty of handcrafted objects still held their value in the eyes of Japanese connoisseurs.

In their products, Japanese artisans may seem to resemble Western artists in their pursuit of aesthetic. However, they would also probably say that they differ significantly in their outlook on life and work. For Western artists, the end product, be it a painting, a sculpture, or something else, stands on its own as an achievement. For Japanese artisans, the end product merely marks a passing point in a life dedicated to the perfection of craftsmanship – even if such perfection may never arrive.

In that sense, most of those we call artists in Japan were more akin to artisans. Katsushika Hokusai (葛飾北斎 1760–1849), the world-famous artist in the *ukiyo-e* genre of highly stylised paintings and woodblock prints, is a case in point. Reputedly, his final words were, 'If only Heaven will give me just another ten years... Just another five more years, then I could become a real painter'.

Japanese artisans are defined through lives committed to their work. It may have something to do with the communal approach the Japanese take to their own identity. In the Western tradition, the artist as an individual comes first – they achieve their goal by expressing their individuality through the art they create. On the other hand, the Japanese artisan achieves their goal over a lifetime through dedication to the work they have chosen.

Looking at the Japanese artisanal tradition, we realise that it has formed the basis of the Japanese work ethic.

日
本
の
生
き
方

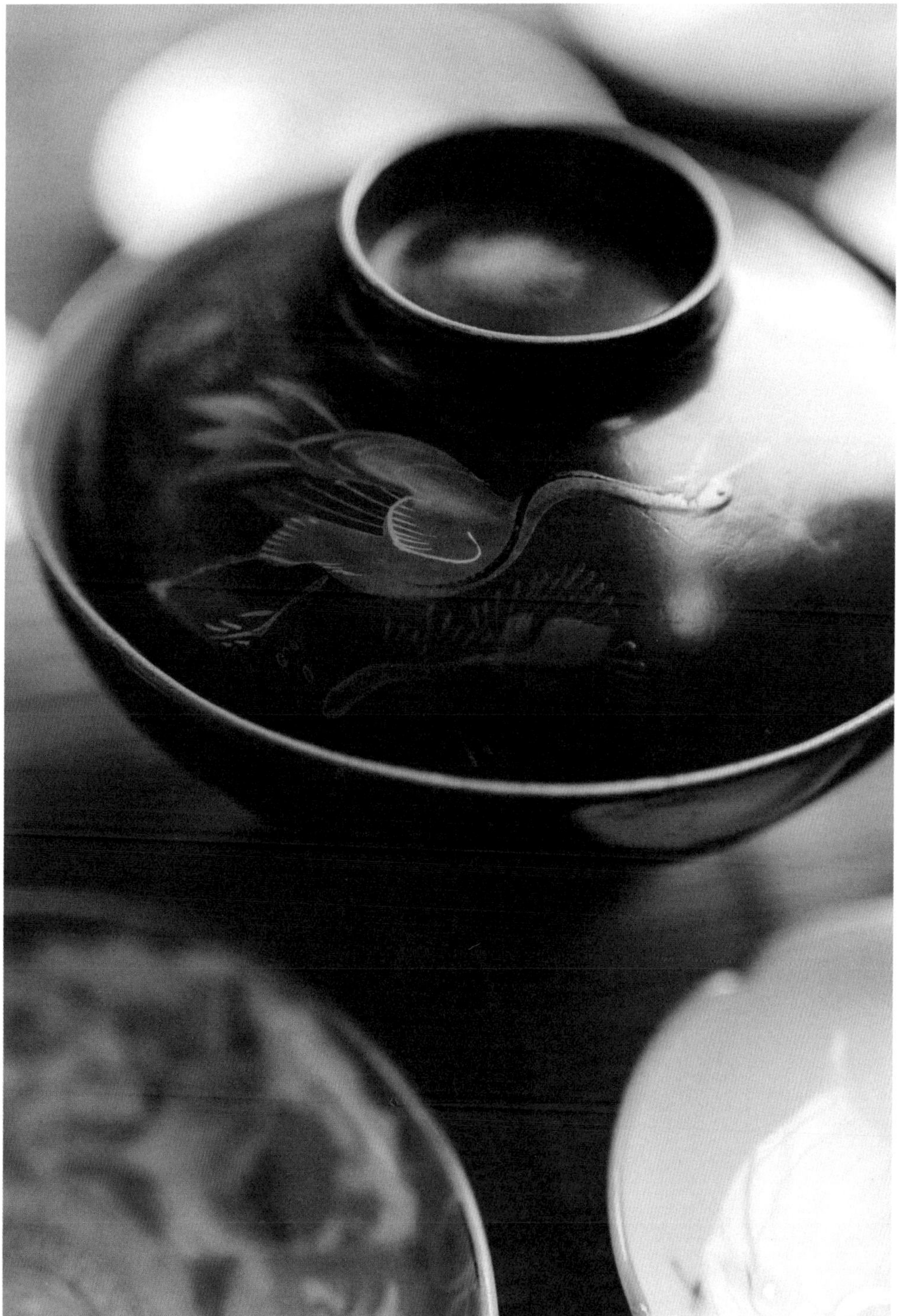

Pottery

As in any other civilisation, pottery can tell us a lot about a country's origins and history. However, for an East Asian country such as Japan, the history of pottery tells a story that is more nuanced and longer than many others. This is because China, as our local hegemon, placed inordinate value and importance on pottery, particularly the porcelain variety. Chinese pieces were so extraordinary that it is still synonymous with porcelain art today.

Japan, as ever, followed China's lead in such cultural matters, and learned to love the fine art of pottery beyond its mere utility. It was, however, an impossible task for provincial Japanese artisans to match the technology and sophistication of the objects coming from China's official imperial kilns. Consequently, fine porcelain pieces were imported to Japan and became highly valued possessions of the wealthy. Japanese artisans had to console themselves with being poor imitators of China's majestic creations.

The tradition of the tea ceremony and its champion, Sen no Rikyū (more of him later), changed perceptions of Japanese pottery forever. Rikyū proclaimed that beauty did not reside only in the flawlessness of imported Chinese porcelain, but also existed in the simple, earthly, unsophisticated pottery of Japanese artisans. His belief was a manifestation of his *wabi-sabi* philosophy of finding beauty and value in imperfection, simplicity and understatement.

Under the patronage of tea masters such as Rikyū, his followers and successors, Japanese pottery found its own aesthetic and confidence, which flourishes to this day. Credit is also due to China, for being such a huge global presence in pottery. To compete, the Japanese had to innovate not just their technology, but their aesthetic philosophy.

日
本
の
生
き
方

Kintsugi

Kintsugi is a traditional method of fixing broken pottery – but one that has become an artform in its own right.

Historically, pottery was vitally important to people. While it was used as everyday essential household tools for storage and cooking, it took an enormous amount of labour and skills to create. Clay had to be found, extracted and carried to the workshop. Kilns were expensive to build and maintain. Charcoal was the eventual fruit of intensive work. Imported Chinese pottery was mainly a veritable treasure due to its artistry. So, naturally, people wanted to be able to mend their precious pots if they broke (this was long before the wastefulness of modern consumerism arrived).

Urushi (漆) – sap from the Chinese lacquer tree – was mainly used for lacquerware, to beautify as well as strengthen woodcrafts. It was also useful as an adhesive. With the advancement of lacquerware technology and aesthetics in the 15th and 16th centuries, fixing pottery with *urushi* also became artistic. Repairers started to decorate the trace of a fracture where *urushi* was applied with colouring agent such as gold or silver powder, making geometric patterns on the finished product. This method was named *kintsugi*, literally meaning 'putting together with gold'.

Appreciation of *kintsugi* was born out of the tradition of the tea ceremony. In particular, Sen no Rikyū, that tea master extraordinaire, praised *kintsugi* as the manifestation of his *wabi-sabi* philosophy. At the risk of oversimplification, Wabi is the way of finding beauty in simple matters. Sabi is the way of finding beauty in reflective, quiet solitude. For Rikyū, *kintsugi* represented the honest presentation of simple artefacts. It told a story: the story of the pot, the loving care its owner had shown to it which necessitated its repair, and the skills and artistry of the repairer. Rikyū resisted the easy love of perfection, symbolised by the imported superior porcelain from China, which was bought with mere wealth. For Rikyū, the imperfection of *kintsugi* pottery was to be cherished for its simple honesty.

Furuta Oribe (古田織部 1544–1615) was a minor warlord who did not shine as a samurai, but became known as an ardent follower of Rikyū and his art of tea ceremony. Impressed by Rikyū's love of *kintsugi*, Oribe started to break his treasured collection of ceramics to make them into *kintsugi*. Informed of Oribe's devotional vandalism, Rikyū reprimanded him, telling him that the true value of *kintsugi* is not in its outward appearance or achieved intentionally through such violent acts. For Rikyū, Oribe's destruction and reconstruction represented contrived and twisted vanity, which was the opposite of what he valued in *kintsugi* and his 'let it be' philosophy.

Robots

According to industry statistics, there were about 1.8 million industrial robots in operation in the world as of the end of 2016 – expected to exceed 3 million by 2020. The number of industrial robots in operation in Japan peaked around the year 2000 with about 380,000 units, and continues to hover over the 300,000 mark.

According to the 2016 statistics, there is a global average of about 74 industrial robots per 10,000 employees. Japan's number is 303 units per 10,000 employees, which puts us fourth in the world for robot density. The gold medal goes to South Korea with 631, the silver to Singapore 488 (a bit of cheating here, as there are only about 24,000 manufacturing sector employees in the city state), and the bronze to Germany, with 309. The USA is catching up with 189 (up from 114 in 2009). However, China has by far the widest margin for growth with only 68 units installed for every 10,000 workers.

In terms of manufacturing the robots, Japan is still the leader, with two of the big four robot manufacturers: Yaskawa Electric Corporation, the market leader, and FANUC Corporation. We are also in the midst of a so-called 'Robot Revolution Initiative', which is a five-year plan to grow our robotics market to over US$21 billion.

The cheerleaders for the Japanese industrial robot industry often claim that we have a natural affinity for robots, citing our long tradition of precision engineering among artisans, as well as our popular *manga* and *anime* culture which contains lots of cyber characters. Leaving the artisan tradition aside, I disagree that our popular culture is robot-friendly.

What the Japanese have done with the robot on a cultural level is to cut down the idea of artificial intelligence (AI) to a size with which we feel comfortable. Our collective imaginations have not really explored the concept to its logical and imaginative limits on its own, such as the science-fiction writer Asimov's robot series, or in the way that Clarke teased us with HAL 9000 in *2001: A Space Odyssey*.

Having said that, the Japanese attitude towards robots is now coming to the next level of evolution. Robots as vehicles is a good enough analogy for the country making leaps and bounds in the automotive industry, but cars are evolving into something more than just vehicles, with self-drive technology just around the corner. Cars are becoming, well, like robots. Robots as tools has been sufficient as a concept for a country relying on its manufacturing sector for export-led economic growth. We face a shortage of labour in the manufacturing sector, so robots in factories are becoming more than just tools. They're becoming robot-colleagues. The Japanese are increasingly aware that we can no longer cut down the concept of a robot to a size that we are comfortable with. We must adapt our lives to suit what robots can offer.

While there is plenty of sensational journalism about robots made to resemble human females as partners for sex-starved men, there is a real need for robots in the care industry, particularly in relation to caring for those suffering from dementia. Human nurses can take physical care of such people – bathing them, changing their clothes and making food (although there are prototype robots that may help with the heavy lifting in the future). What human workers are less well equipped for is constant communication with dementia sufferers. The repetitive or meandering conversations with those with damaged short-term memory function is psychologically taxing for a caregiver. AI-powered devices are now being tested in these situations, as they will never tire from endlessly looping chit-chat and can help sustain a conversation.

We are slowly yet surely experiencing the dawning realisation that AI and its mechanical representations are creeping into our daily lives. This is not only irreversible, but permanent and necessary. It may be a manifestation of this very realisation that we are beginning to accept being entertained and served by robots in places like restaurants and hotels.

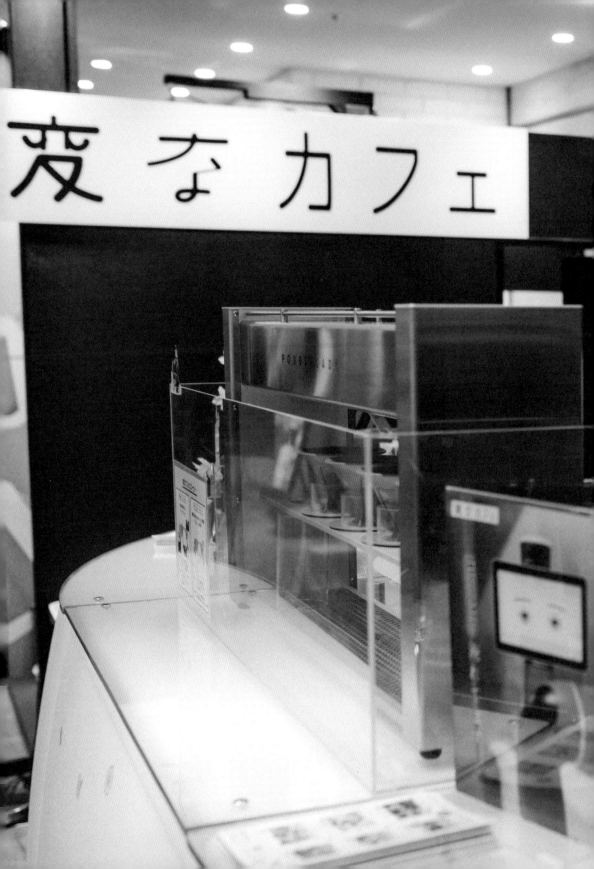

At the Table

The impact of tea

Tea is arguably China's greatest gift to the world. The Chinese are quick to remind us about all the other things they have, and are supposed to have, invented – but while the jury may still be out on, say, the benefits of gunpowder, tea is universally liked.

It was first introduced to Japan around the 9th century at the height of the glorious Tang dynasty, one of those many periods when all of Asia looked to China as the font of civilisation and culture. However, once the Tang dynasty went into decline and Chinese things went out of fashion, the first tea-drinking boom in Japanese history waned.

Tea's renaissance in Japan began towards the end of the 12th century, thanks to a monk called Eisai (栄西), who studied the latest Buddhist trends in China's Song dynasty. When he returned to Japan, he came with the seeds and sapling of a tea tree, and the latest trend in Buddhist teaching, Zen Buddhism.

The powerful merchant class of Sakai collectively ran an independent, autonomous city much like Venice. One member of that class was Sen no Rikyū (千利休 1522–1591), considered the founder of the tea ceremony tradition that we know today. He practised the new art of the tea ceremony and developed it, through his passion for Zen Buddhism, into an art form.

Rikyū's tea ceremony, in its essence, is the organising of a party. The host invites the guests to enjoy tea made by that host. However, all the processes of organising the simple act of enjoying tea together must be carried out along the basis of aesthetics rooted in Zen Buddhism. The invitation, handwritten with a traditional Japanese brush, must be pleasing both to read and look at. The guests arrive at the appointed place to observe the garden fully prepared, but not artificially manicured like a flower garden. Zen Buddhism sees beauty in the harmony between nature and the host's intent to welcome and please the guests.

The meals provided to the guests before the tea is served are also prepared according to Zen monks' practices. They are called *kaiseki-ryōri* (懐石料理), which literally means 'cuisine of stone held to the body', recalling the tale of meditating Zen monks holding heated stones close to their stomachs to alleviate hunger. The meal cannot be a gluttonous feast, because Zen Buddhism abhors excess. Ingredients may be rare and precious, but the presentation must not be ravishing. The guests are then guided to a teahouse, which is a small building symbolising a corner of the universe in which the host and the guests feel the closeness of each other. The teahouse can only be entered through a small entrance, forcing the guests to kneel, thereby removing any pretence of social hierarchy and overbearing mannerism in anticipation of equal companionship with the host and other guests. The furniture is basic and bare, with one piece of art or nature, perhaps a flower, adorning the wall to symbolise the theme of the event or a connection with the world outside the small room in which all now sit. The water boils in a simple cast-iron kettle over a fireplace cut in the floor, and the tea is prepared in a ceramic bowl. The Japanese had admired and valued flawless ceramics created

日
本
の
生
き
方

in China, but Rikyū encouraged his followers to see the beauty in simple, Japanese-made pots. He also encouraged value in asymmetry and flaws, which are more honest reflections of nature.

The art of this style of tea ceremony has been growing stronger ever since Rikyū began. It is practised by men and women, young and old, to this day. An art critic once called it the 'art of peace' which has been the source of spiritual nourishment for the Japanese people and their arts.

Dashi: the umami of everything

Truth be told, we Japanese should doff our caps to China for anything culinary. They have been at it for over 4,000 years. Constant effort has been poured into their pursuit of gastronomy, coupled with the search for a healthy diet. Chinese vocabularies are full of cooking-related words.

Compared to this cooking titan on our doorstep, Japan's food traditions are naturally modest. That said, nothing compares to home cooking, and we take pride in what we have to offer.

Chief among our proud traditions is the discovery of *umami* (旨味). *Umami* is usually translated into English as 'savoury taste', but it is so much more than that. It is the taste in foods that is neither sweet, sour, salty, nor bitter, but nevertheless forms an essential part of a full palate. It comes from the variety of amino acid combinations.

Japanese people use various ingredients to extract *umami*. Usually, we boil sea kelp seaweed (*kombu* 昆布), or dried bonito fish (*katsuobushi* 鰹節) to make a broth which we call *dashi* (出汁). *Dashi*, literally meaning 'extracted soup', is full of *umami* and is used as a base in a number of dishes.

We have been using *dashi* for centuries, but *umami* was only discovered and scientifically analysed at the beginning of the 20th century by chemistry professor Kikunae Ikeda (池田菊苗 1864–1936). He co-founded a company to produce the *umami* seasoning called Ajinomoto – the original producer of monosodium glutamate (MSG).

Compared to other tastes, such as saltiness and sweetness, *umami* is subtle. Perhaps for this reason, it is regarded as a sign of a sophisticated palate to appreciate it.

Sake: old drink, new industry

When Japan was first described in the Chinese official chronicle in the 3rd century, it noted that Japanese people liked to drink. They got that right (although they left the geographical location of Japan rather vague). So, it appears that the Japanese knew how to make sake (referred to as rice wine, it in fact more closely resembled beer then) from rice quite early on and it was drunk by all in large quantities.

In the Heian period (8th–12th century), the court in Kyoto brewed its own sake, like Emperor's Own. But the better ones were made by the priests in temples, Japanese Bishop's Brew if you like. Nothing, it seems, makes for better alcohol than holy thoughts.

The nationwide sake-making boom had to wait until the Kamakura period (12th–14th century), when the advance in agricultural output made it possible for the farmers to set aside an extra yield of rice for sake making.

As sake production requires a steady rice supply, a distribution and sales network, brewers became prototype capitalists. They were the wealthy local landowner types who could produce and/or buy up the necessary rice. The brewing work that took place during wintertime following the harvest also provided good opportunities for tenant farmers during the slack season, and some of them became specialist master sake makers, known as Toji (杜氏), hired for their expert skills by the highest bidder.

The end of the Second World War ushered in the dark period for sake when cheap, bad quality and sometimes downright dangerous alcohol made its rounds on the black market, bringing down sake's reputation with it. The makers did their best to recover from this nadir, through fairs and competition between brands. Scientific advances also helped.

Although the economic environment surrounding sake makers is not getting any easier, it is safe to say that we are now drinking a better quality sake than at any other time in history. Nevertheless, apart from a group of major producers in Nada and Kyoto, sake makers still tend to have small, local businesses that are vulnerable to any whim of economic adversity.

Sake can be divided into categories of Junmai, Ginjo and Dai-Ginjo, depending on the amount of polishing rice goes through at the beginning of the process. These categories are, in fact, of recent invention and are part of a sales effort by sake makers to differentiate their products. Although Ginjo and Dai-Ginjo were prized at first for their clearer tastes, achieved through extensive rice polishing, the fickleness of consumers is always swinging to and fro and some prefer Junmai for its characterful palate.

Small sake businesses are energetically selling their products to foreign markets with a 'never say die' attitude.

In a way, for the resilience and innovation of all involved, sake is a typically Japanese product that we can responsibly be proud of, without the need for moderation.

Pesco-vegetarian Japan

Somehow, livestock farming didn't take off in Japan until modern times. The consumption of meat was limited to fish, chicken and occasional game. This is very odd considering that the Chinese table is not complete without pork or some other kind of meat, and that, historically speaking, the Japanese more often than not followed where the Chinese led.

The absence of meat from traditional Japanese food culture is most probably due to Buddhist influence. Although there was never a religious taboo about eating meat, Buddhist monks thought it better to refrain, believing that too much protein led to impure thoughts, which were a hindrance to their meditative spiritual lifestyle. Often, you will see a sign at the gates of temples saying, '不許葷酒入山門' – 'No garlic, other strong vegetables, meat, fish or alcohol is allowed to enter the temple gate'.

The prohibition was a mere policy statement for those leading religious lives, but it set the standard for the rest of society. It appears that non-religious Japanese people could not resist alcohol and fish, but drew the line at eating meat in their search for cleaner living.

In times of war and civil strife, such as in the Age of the Warring States, these prohibitions were loosened, and people hunted for game, mainly boar and deer. They had to eat them to survive. As soon as peace returned, people refrained from eating meat on the basis of social norm.

Fukuzawa Yukichi (福沢諭吉 1835–1901) was an influential scholar and proponent of Western civilisation towards the end of the Edo period and the start of the Meiji Reformation. He studied Western medicine in Osaka between 1855 and 1858, and wrote vividly about this period of his life in a famous autobiography. Fukuzawa recalls that there was a place serving beef hotpot in a certain part of Osaka where the underclasses lived and other people avoided. Priding themselves on being above such prejudices as scholars of modern science, Fukuzawa and his fellow students frequented this place – but they were always greeted by disapproving neighbours upon their return, because of the smell of cooked meat they carried back home.

One of the side-effects of Japanese abstention from meat eating was physical. In the 250 years of peace under the Tokugawa shogunate, people's aversion to meat meant that the average height of the Japanese people decreased significantly. When Commodore Perry of the US East India Squadron came knocking in 1853, many samurai were called on to protect the coastline around Edo Bay. However, when they tried to put on their family heirloom armour, many found that their bodies were too small.

With the Meiji Reformation, the adoption of Western civilisation and, to a lesser degree, Western culture, eating meat became fashionable, and people quickly shrugged off their inhibitions. This means that, for the first time in their history, Japanese people have been eating meat on a continuous basis for 150 years. In the meantime, the average height of the Japanese people, both male and female, has increased by almost 20cm. Historically, we are the tallest Japanese. By and large, meat-eating appears to have been good for us, although it may have been achieved at the expense of a meditative spiritual lifestyle.

日
本
の
生
き
方

From fast food to main course

Tempura (天麩羅), that quintessentially Japanese deep-fried dish, actually has its origins in Portugal. The cooking method of deep-frying with a batter arrived in Japan in the 16th century with the Jesuits – and while they were persecuted, we kept their cooking.

At the time, cooking oil was generally made from sesame seeds, and was so expensive that *tempura* was a food reserved for the rich.

As the price of cooking oil came down with increased production during the Edo period, *tempura* became popular, particularly in the new capital, Edo, where it was sold by street vendors. It was one of three 'Edo foods' that originated and were popularised in Edo, alongside *sushi* and *soba* noodles.

Tempura as a street food was usually made with vegetables, especially root vegetables such as lotus root and sweet potato. Seafood such as shrimp and eel caught in Edo Bay was also used (and was known as *Edomae* [江戸前], meaning 'in front of Edo'). The ingredients were coated in a batter of egg and flour, then deep-fried in hot sesame oil in front of eager customers.

It was only much later, around the end of Tokugawa shogunate in the mid-19th century, that *tempura* vendors began to have their own restaurants. It wasn't until at least 1923 that *tempura* spread beyond the city now called Tokyo, when the Great Kantō earthquake destroyed the restaurants of many *tempura* chefs, who moved to Osaka and elsewhere to sell their food.

If you go to a specialist *tempura* restaurant in Tokyo (not so much outside the capital), you can still see traces of the former street-vendor style of service. You choose from the ingredients on display and tell the *tempura* chef behind the counter which ingredients you want to be fried. The knack of the chef is to control the oil's temperature in accordance with the ingredients so the *tempura* is fried with the core of the ingredients remaining soft and flavourful.

As mentioned above, *sushi* (鮨) also originates from Edo. However, a wider definition of *sushi* as a method of preserving fish with rice using vinegar existed long before that.

What happened in Edo was the invention of *nigiri sushi* (握り寿司), where a piece of fish is served on top of a vinegar-flavoured rice ball. In other words, *sushi* as it is globally known today.

Unlike *tempura*, *sushi* only became popular in Edo in, it is generally believed, the first half of the 19th century, but it quickly caught on. At first, the rice portion of *sushi* was much bigger than it is today, and it was regarded as a quick snack, or even fast food.

The availability of fresh *Edomae* seafood was the important factor in the early days of *nigiri sushi* – nationwide popularity had to wait for the introduction of the refrigerator. As improved refrigeration techniques arrived, the ingredients used for *sushi* became more numerous. At first, they were almost exclusively the types of fish that could be caught in nearby seas, such as horse mackerel, sardine and bonito. Modern staples, such as tuna, came more recently as they became easier to transport and store.

日
本
の
生
き
方

Sushi, like *tempura*, developed into a main-course meal served at restaurants through the efforts of chefs who were eager for a value-added business model. This resulted in more fashionable *sushi* restaurants that charge exorbitant prices for what is essentially a simple food that started life as a snack. Cynics complain about this inflationary phenomenon, but one must admit that there is something deeply alluring and Japanese about the minimalist charm of *sushi* and *sushi* restaurants that loosen our wallets.

Foreign foods gone native

One of the benefits of not having a world-beating cuisine of its own is that the Japanese have adopted many foreign foods as their own. *Tempura*, as mentioned previously, is a chief example, having been introduced to Japan by the Portuguese. Here are some other Japanese foods that actually came from further afield.

RAMEN (拉麺) Now regarded as one of Japan's major culinary exports, *ramen* actually originated in China. When Japanese soldiers returned from China after the Second World War, many brought with them recipes for Chinese noodles. One of those was for *ramen*, noodles made from flour and brine. At the same time, the US was providing large quantities of flour to the Japanese population by way of aid, as well as marketing for their agricultural products. The Japanese were not ready to become bread-eaters overnight, but these new noodles became a hit with starving people who needed quick energy boosts for reconstruction work.

TONKATSU (豚カツ) This deep-fried pork fillet was introduced at the end of the 19th century and made popular by a restaurant in Tokyo's Ginza district, called Renga-tei (煉瓦亭). Its roots are distinctly European: French *côtelette*, Milanese *cotoletta* and German *schnitzel*. Various methods of deep-frying evolved – some involved frying thick fillet slowly, while others involved frying relatively thinner pieces quickly. Shredded cabbage as the standard side dish was also invented at Renga-tei.

AN-PAN (あんパン) Bread (*pan*, from the French *pain*) with a sweet filling made from red bean paste. Yasubei Kimura (木村安兵衛 1817–1889), a brilliant innovator and pioneering baker, was trying to popularise bread in Japan. In 1874, he came up with the idea of putting *anko* (あんこ), a sweet red bean paste and staple of Japanese confectionery, inside bread. It became a sensation when the Meiji emperor gave the bakery an imperial warrant. That bakery, Kimuraya, is still in Ginza and still hugely popular.

CASTELLA (カステラ) A sponge cake made from flour, sugar and eggs that was brought to Japan with the Jesuits in the 16th century. The name *castella* is a bit of mystery, though. Some say it comes from the Spanish region of Castilla, while others say it is derived from the Portuguese word for castle, *castelo*. There are *castella* bakeries in Nagasaki whose history goes back to the 17th century.

CURRY RICE (カレーライス) Japanese curry is nothing like any dish from India. Curry was introduced to Japan around 1873, taken from British naval recipes (thick, stew-like dishes) and served in the Imperial Japanese Navy. By the beginning of the 20th century, curry became popular with the general public and continues to be a family staple.

日本の生き方

日 本 の 生 き 方

Why we have so many Michelin stars

Apparently, the American chef Anthony Bourdain cannot get enough of Japan as a foodie destination – and not just for Japanese cuisine. Tokyo continues to boast more Michelin stars than any other city in the world.

Historically, the Japanese have been a modest bunch when it comes to eating. As discussed previously, we had been long under the Buddhist influence of avoiding meat, and the sumptuousness of a table was something to avoid, in line with the stoic virtues of samurai ethics.

In the immediate aftermath of the Second World War, the whole population of Japan was starving. City-dwellers survived on the black market and going to the countryside to barter their possessions directly with farmers for food. The Japanese emerged from this dire situation in the 1950s, but food remained as an obsession in our collective psyche. Being a gourmet was once thought to be vulgar but now became a legitimate pursuit. Everybody became a food critic, and nothing contributes more to a standard of cooking than discerning foodies.

From the supply side, Japanese artisanal tradition seeped into the food industry. There had always been a tradition of master and apprentice in conventional Japanese cuisine, but it spread to all other food categories. Aspiring chefs competed to work as apprentices to top chefs, and then sought further training in France, Italy and other motherlands of their chosen cuisine. After a few years of overseas training, they returned to Japan to open their own restaurants and became new 'masters' in their own right to foster the next generation.

The size and growth of Tokyo as a megalopolis also helped these new restaurant owners. In places like Hong Kong, with limited size and concentration of real estate, landlords hike up rents as soon as a tenant restaurant becomes successful. As a result, customers are paying more for the rent than the food whereas Tokyo is kinder to start-up chefs in that respect. There have been a few big restaurant franchises trying to disrupt the cycle with slick interiors and the efficiency of centralised food production, as opposed to food being made by a chef in residence. Nevertheless, Japanese foodies tend to prefer smaller establishments with owner-chefs firmly in charge of operations.

All in all, we now have an ideal ecosystem in Japan for high-quality eateries to thrive. The media, from TV to publishing, ceaselessly streams information to fuel competition. It seems that Michelin stars will continue to shine above Tokyo for the foreseeable future.

Wagyu: a misguided obsession?

Meat really only entered Japanese cuisine recently. It was regarded as unclean and undesirable, due to the influence of clean-living Buddhist monks with little demand for a protein-rich diet.

Everything changed with the introduction of Western culture. The European way of life was regarded as cool, modern and advanced. The Western food too acquired an air of sophistication and desirability.

Of more serious concern was the Japanese physique. Through centuries of abstention, the average height of Japanese people hit a statistical low in the 19th century. At the time, the new government was busy establishing a modern army to match those of the Western powers. Guns and ships from Europe were easily purchased, but they could do little to improve the size of Japan's soldiers, who looked diminutive next to their European counterparts. The Japanese diet had to be improved.

Out of vogue *and* necessity, meat-eating was taken to the mainstream.

Centuries-old tastes were difficult to change. Apart from early adopters, people still had difficulties consuming meat, especially beef, as the cooked smell and taste was not associated with good food. Therefore, initial efforts to adopt beef into Japanese cuisine took the form of subduing its smell and taste.

Admiral Tōgō Heihachirō (東郷平八郎 1848–1934) became famous as a victor of the Battle of Tsushima (1905) when his fleet destroyed Imperial Russia's Baltic Fleet during the critical phase of the Russo-Japan War. In the 1870s, he spent his youth studying in Britain, and when he returned to Japan, he spoke of a tasty English dish called 'beef stew'. Eager to please a promising naval officer, a cook tried to recreate the food from Tōgō's description. The end result was what is known in Japan to this day as *nikujaga* (肉じゃが), or 'beef and potatoes'. It is a dish smothered in *dashi* broth, soy sauce, sugar and sweet *sake*. It is tasty, but nothing like a British beef stew, and the natural taste of the beef is hidden by the added Japanese flavours.

Another early Japanese recipe using beef, which is also still popular today, is *sukiyaki* (すきやき). It is made by boiling thinly sliced beef with vegetables in a soup made, again, from soy sauce, sugar and sweet *sake*.

In both *nikujaga* and *sukiyaki*, only thin slices of beef are used, and the Japanese flavouring is used to undermine the natural flavour of the meat. By the time the beef is cooked, its flavour has drained into the broth.

This is not the way to treat good beef.

As the Japanese got used to the smell and taste of beef, they became familiar with actual European styles of cooking it, such as roasting and grilling. By eating roast beef and steaks, the Japanese began to appreciate the meat for its unique taste.

To respond to this change in the palate, Japanese meat producers began to raise their cattle to produce beef with fat that would not drain into the broth when Japanese cooking methods were used. So began the fad for 'marbled' beef, in which the fat content of the meat is not only increased, but it is meshed into the muscle fibre, giving a cut the appearance of red and white marbled stone.

In pursuit of added value, farmers in Japan have gone to extraordinary lengths to create fatty beef. They limited their cattle's movement by keeping them in sheds, fed them special foods, and sometimes made them drink beer. They played them Mozart, and even analysed the DNA of breeds for their propensity to produce marbled beef.

One thing they forgot to do was to protect their intellectual property. Wagyū (和牛) means 'Japanese beef', but the name was used by Australian farmers who were keen to exploit this consumer trend by producing their own marbled beef and branding it as 'Wagyu'. To counter this, Japanese producers started using the names of their own localities to brand their meat, such as 'Kobe beef' or 'Yonezawa beef'.

There is an argument that the fad for Wagyu has gone too far. A certain amount of unsaturated fat in beef is beneficial, but current levels are excessive, and the methods used to create such levels are inhumane. In any event, as explained, the trend started from a misguided approach to cooking beef. Wagyu beef with excessive fat levels makes for a terrible steak – you don't want to eat steak swimming in its own fat.

Chinya (ちんや), one of the oldest sukiyaki restaurants in Japan, and located in the Asakusa area of Tokyo, recently made a declaration entitled 'Teki-sashi sengen', or 'declaration of appropriate fat levels'. Stating that they value beef for its taste, and not just for the level of fat contained in it. The excessive fat does not equate to good flavour. I wholeheartedly welcome this move, and not just because I loved Chinya's sukiyaki in the first place.

Japanese whisky

The story of how whisky arrived in Japan is a well-known one in the country, made even more familiar by having been made into a popular TV series.

Masataka Taketsuru (竹鶴政孝 1894–1979) went to Glasgow in 1918 to study chemistry, and later apprenticed with several Scottish distilleries. He returned to Japan with his Scottish wife Rita and started to produce whisky with a company that is now known as Suntory. He later started his own company, Nikka. Whiskies produced by both Suntory and Nikka are now regarded as being among the best in the world.

One of Suntory's distilleries is in Yamazaki (山崎), near Kyoto. It was chosen for its water, which has been known for centuries for its quality. Visiting the Yamazaki distillery the immaculate care taken to maintain the whisky casks is most impressive. Casks make a significant contribution to the colour and flavour of whisky, and their maintenance is time-consuming and expensive.

The problem with the whisky business is that you cannot immediately increase production, even if your product becomes popular. Higher production only materialises in more output a decade or so down the line. It requires patience and humility.

It was lucky for Japanese whisky that its pioneer distillers had these qualities in abundance. They knew they were attempting something difficult, and respected the original whisky makers of Scotland and their traditions. Humility did not allow the new challengers to cut corners, and kept them on their toes in new innovations. The quality we see in Japanese whiskies today owes much to this.

The first distillers also respected the consumer in introducing this foreign spirit. Drinking highly alcoholic spirits was not a Japanese habit and people were slow to take to whisky drinking. When the quality of other alcohol beverages plummeted in the poverty of the post-war period, whisky makers saw their chance, and the popularity of the beverage grew alongside a recovering Japan.

In a way, Japanese whiskies are now at a crossroads. The quality of the product and the producers' diligence have led, over a period of time, to success that has coincided with the emergence of Japan as an economic power. They are now in soul-searching mode to ensure their continuing success. As an example, after Suntory's *Hibiki* blended whisky won a prestigious prize, it became difficult to find. In response, Suntory made the bottles smaller. The move was condemned by the world's whisky aficionados as a quick money-making scheme.

The new situation poses a challenge for Japanese whisky makers, not just to maintain the high quality they have achieved, but to nurture their brands. That requires more than just humility, but a lot of patience and self-control.

Robatayaki and teppanyaki

Japanese communal eating habits have been a tame affair. We were light years behind the Chinese in sumptuousness – while an emperor in China could command all the delicacies under the sun to be assembled at his table, the Japanese had to make do with locally available ingredients. During the period in the 8th century when Chinese fashion reigned supreme at the Japanese imperial court, it was briefly fashionable to hold a 'Chinese style' feast. The fad soon died down – apparently, the Japanese didn't find sitting on the chairs, *à la chinoise*, agreeable.

Japanese dining style has been influenced by the tea ceremony, which was, in turn, influenced by Zen Buddhism and its tradition of *shōjin ryōri* (精進料理), meaning 'devotional cuisine'. Zen monks eat sparingly, barely enough to sustain themselves in their contemplative lifestyle. It is not so much feasting as dining on rations. It is certainly healthy, if far from fun.

All this means is that communal eating as entertainment came into the Japanese consciousness rather late. *Robatayaki* (炉端焼き) is a style of dining where food, usually fish, shellfish and vegetables, is slow-grilled on skewers over an open charcoal fire in front of diners, rather like a barbeque. It is modelled on the country lifestyle, where family members gather around a hearth to eat by the fireside. The style originated at a restaurant in Sendai in the 1950s.

Teppanyaki (鉄板焼き) is a method where food is grilled on a hot iron plate, also in front of diners. This style was made popular by a steakhouse in Kobe right after the war, and became a hit in the USA with the Benihana restaurant chain founded by Japanese entrepreneur Hiroaki 'Rocky' Aoki (青木廣彰) in the 1960s. It was re-imported to Japan following its success Stateside.

Both *robatayaki* and *teppanyaki* introduced showmanship and, consequently, fun into the Japanese dining experience. Cooks in *robatayaki* and *teppanyaki* restaurants entertain guests with their deft handling of ingredients.

It is telling that both styles were born in the period right after the war, when the Japanese were emerging from the chronic shortage of food. With the memory and fear of starvation receding, people took to eating as an easy way of appreciating the return of peace and enjoying the fruits of modest prosperity. As a result, we have added a new page to our culinary culture.

Life Outside

Hiking

If horse racing is the sport of British kings, then Japan's royal sport must surely be hiking.

Kunimi (国見), literally meaning 'looking at the kingdom', was a tradition in ancient Japan. On certain auspicious days, rulers went to the highest points of their domains to look over the lands they ruled by way of giving blessings for good harvests, and so on.

Naruhito, the Crown Prince of Japan (皇太子徳仁親王) who at the time of writing is due to become emperor on 1 May 2019, has taken *kunimi* to new heights. He is an avid hiker, and since the age of five, has climbed about 170 peaks throughout Japan.

Some criticise Naruhito's hobby. He is inevitably accompanied on his hikes by bodyguards and hangers-on. With the press corps also tagging along, his groups are thought to number about 100 people. When Naruhito is hiking, routes get congested and ordinary hikers are affected. On the plus side, the Crown Prince leaves in his wake a suspiciously well-manicured trail. The route signs are fixed, mountain huts are renovated, and public conveniences are immaculate.

With or without His Imperial Highness' warrant, hiking is a popular pursuit. There are several good mountains within easy reach of Tokyo, and even famous peaks above the 2,000m mark are no further than a day's journey away via well-connected train and local bus services.

Apart from the ancient practice of *kunimi*, mountain climbing has been historically linked with religious training. Some monks commit themselves to 100 or 1,000 days of continuous climbing of holy peaks as part of their devotion and search for Nirvana. Religious hermits in mountains known as *yamabushi* (山伏) are also following a religious tradition in which people don the *yamabushi*'s particular clothing and stay in the mountains, bearing the hardship of living outdoors and being exposed to the elements as physical training for religious purposes. Even now, ordinary people take part in *yamabushi* experiences for a limited period as a hobby or lifestyle choice.

Mainstream hikers are a more easy-going bunch. Nevertheless, they share their enthusiasm with those ancient traditions, going to the mountains to escape the busyness of their daily lives. The clean, fresh air of mountain forests is sufficient reward. *Shinrin-yoku* (森林浴) is the term the Japanese created for it, literally meaning 'forest bathing'. They say that 'bathing' in the fresh air of forests has positive physical effects. Nobody could argue against that.

Sometimes, especially around autumn and its colours, the mountains get too congested. The experience may be far from the serenity that one seeks. Still, you realise that people are a lot nicer in the peaks. Strangers exchange greetings as they pass each other, sometimes giving those ascending a few words of encouragement. It feels as if Japan's great outdoors has the magic to bring out the better in people. For me, that feels like a true religious experience. As the saying goes, 'You do not go to mountains to be enlightened. Rather, you go to mountains because you are enlightened.'

Adopted national sports: baseball, football and... rugby?

The Japanese have always had an affinity towards sport as physical exercise thanks to the martial arts tradition. What was lacking in the past was the concept of sport as a game – any kind of fun, basically. Those dedicating themselves to swordsmanship through *kendo*, or martial artistry through *judo* and other close-combat disciplines, were a stoic bunch, seeking satisfaction from nothing other than blood, sweat, toil and tears, in and of themselves. So, when an American teacher called Horace Wilson (1843–1927) introduced the game of baseball to his Japanese students in the 1870s, he basically dropped a spark in the tinderbox.

Baseball became wildly popular, and it happened very quickly. The game taught the Japanese that sporting activity could be fun, and it also opened our eyes to the joy of team sports.

Waseda University, one of the major private universities in Japan, sent its baseball team to the USA in 1905 at the height of the Russo-Japanese War. The team brought back the latest American techniques and coaching methods. In those early days, the annual two-game series between Waseda and Keio Universities was regarded as the pinnacle of Japanese baseball. The 1906 series saw the universities sharing a win each, but the deciding game had to be cancelled due to the frenzy of the fans, culminating in threats being made not only to the student-players, but also to the umpires.

There were those who regarded baseball with disdain. From the stoic heights of Japanese martial arts, baseball seemed like an elaborate version of the game of tag – there was just too much fun and not enough suffering. However, baseball prevailed. The first professional baseball team was founded in 1920, and the professional league was established in 1936. Baseball continues to be the most popular sport in Japan.

Football (or soccer) has been played in Japan since the 1870s. There are many stories and theories about the true starting point of the game in Japan, with many expats' social clubs in port cities such as Yokohama and Kobe organising matches at random. In any event, it gradually spread through schools in the late 19th and early 20th centuries.

Unlike baseball, which was a young game even at the time of its introduction to Japan, football already had a relatively long history, so the Japanese newcomers had a tough time catching up with the rest of the world and suffered several humiliating international defeats.

In 1993, the Japanese Professional Football League, known as the 'J.League', was established. With strong leadership from the Japan Football Association, it re-established football's place by founding a vibrant professional domestic league which started to feed elite players into the national team. That side started winning international matches and became a regular participant in the FIFA World Cup. Football is now the third most popular sport in Japan after baseball and *sumo*.

日
本
の
生
き
方

Just like baseball and football, rugby has been played in Japan since the 1870s, but mainly among expat residents in the early days. A difference in physical size between the Japanese and the expats obviously seemed to have played a part in the Japanese taking part themselves slowly and relunctantly. However, in 1899, Edward Bramwell Clarke (1874–1934), a teacher born in Yokohama to English parents, introduced the game to his students at Keio University with help from Ginnosuke Tanaka (田中銀之助 1873–1933), a businessman who had studied in England and played the game there.

From the 1920s, rugby steadily became a popular sport through inter-collegiate games, but the disaster struck around sixty years later, when Japan was invited to participate in the first Rugby World Cup (RWC) in 1987.

Japan has been taking part in the RWC ever since, but had been tossed around in defeat for three decades, most painfully in a 145–17 thrashing at the hands of New Zealand's All Blacks in 1995. (There was a 52–8 victory against Zimbabwe in 1991, and a tie against Canada in 2007.)

Japanese rugby had to wait until 2012 for its true awakening, when Australian Eddie Jones was appointed as head coach to the national side. With the sense of pride in representing the nation instilled by Jones, the players managed to pull off a shock 34-32 win against South Africa in the 2015 RWC, and two other wins in the pool stage.

With the 2019 RWC to be held in Japan, rugby's popularity is increasing. How far this momentum will carry the game forward into the future remains to be seen.

日
本
の
生
き
方

Sumo: in praise of the big men

These days, sumō (相撲) is in limbo. It cannot make up its mind whether it is a sport or cultural event steeped in tradition. Like any other wrestling-type sports found all over the world, sumo's history goes back to the mythical age. In the Shinto religion, the sun goddess Amaterasu's people came to a Japan that was already populated by indigenous gods. Takemikazuchi, one of Amaterasu's newcomers, challenged the indigenous god Takeminakata to a bout of sumo. The former overwhelmed the latter, who fled to the province of Shinano and died from the wounds sustained in the bout. Takeminakata became the god of the Suwa Shrine (諏訪神社), which still thrives.

During the period in which the emperors ruled Japan, sumo tournaments became a form of entertainment and an event in the court calendar. An emperor, or his court, actively looked for big, strong men throughout Japan to serve as professional sumo wrestlers, and the annual tournament was held in summer in front of him. It is thought that such sumo tournaments were dedicated to gods as prayers for good harvest.

As the power of emperors and their courts declined, so did sumo as a ceremonial spectacle. It survived as a recreational activity, but professional sumo wrestlers found it difficult to make a living after traditional sponsors and organisers of tournaments had left the scene. Oda Nobunaga (織田信長1534–1582), a famous warlord from the Age of the Warring States, emerged as sumo's saviour. He was already a big fan, and introduced rules and a structure of his own.

Under the peace guaranteed by the Tokugawa shogunate, popular culture flourished, and sumo became entertainment for the masses. Professional sumo wrestlers were once more in demand and the promoters of tournaments were keen to give events proper pomp and circumstance. A ranking system was introduced, with titles we recognise today, such as yokozuna (横綱), or 'grand champions'.

Professional sumo organisers began to add more pageantry and splendour to their tournaments with referees starting to wear more anachronistic costumes. The promotion of sumo wrestlers, especially to the top rank of yokozuna, is an archaic affair decided by a committee made up of the selected 'great and good' members of the Japanese establishment. Increasingly, sumo has become less like a sport and more like a collection of traditions which are, in reality, of modern origin.

Recently, sumo wrestlers have begun to get bigger meaning bouts are often won by the largest competitor, with little room for skilful wrestlers to shine. There has also been a decline in home-grown talent, and many top-class participants now come from Mongolia. Fifteen-day tournaments six times a year, which became standard only in 1949, are taking their physical toll on the wrestlers. There are persistent rumours of bout-fixing among wrestlers to save their rankings and their bodies.

In short, professional sumo is in a bit of a quandary in this modern context. So many elements are screaming for reform and improvement but it is hindered by anachronistic tendencies to maintain the cultural traditions. There seems to be no easy answer.

Let's go to Kyoto

JR Tōkai (JR東海) is one of the Japanese railway companies and runs the *Shinkansen* 'bullet train' service between Tokyo and Kyoto. In 1993, it ran an ad campaign promoting the former capital city with the catchphrase, 'Yes, let's go to Kyoto'. It was so successful that the same catchphrase continues to this day, prompting lots of holidaymakers to jump on the super-fast train to satisfy their wanderlust.

When the bullet train was being developed in the early 1960s, the World Bank loaned US$80 million for the project. There was scepticism that train services dedicated only to passenger transport would be successful. Such pessimism was proved wrong. In its first year operating between Tokyo and Osaka, the bullet train carried an average of 84,000 passengers per day, which rose rapidly to around 231,000 passengers per day in its fifth year.

The reason why tourism is such big part of leisure time in Japan is, in my opinion, because our lifestyle is very sedate and confined. Back when agriculture was the country's main industry, work in the fields required labourers' constant attention. People were tied to their land and had little time to venture outside their small villages. Even with the emergence of commercial activities and the rise in urban population, mostly in the Edo period, workers had no weekend respite as we know it today. Holidays were restricted to a few days in summer for *Obon* (お盆) to commemorate ancestors, and between three and seven days to celebrate the new year. Under such claustrophobic restrictions, people yearned to travel as an escape from everyday life.

In the Edo period, the most popular destination for those fortunate enough to have both leave and the necessary funds was the Ise Grand Shrine (伊勢神宮) dedicated to the aforementioned goddess Amaterasu. It took about two weeks on foot (horses were not available to commoners) to get from Edo to Ise, and then on to Kyoto. The Tōkaidō coastal route had (and still does have) amazing views, particularly of Mt Fuji, as well as hostel towns known for their seafood dotted along the route.

People needed to roam. The destination itself had only a nominal purpose. It was the journey that mattered, as an escape from the reality of life at home. These factors remain true today. In modern-day Japan, most people are still tied up in life-long employment, and the everyday rat race has become not so much a race but congestion. People needing a short break from reality take a weekend holiday. Kyoto is a good destination. It is convenient and there is always something to see. But people cannot stray too far and must return to a dull, yet comfortable life at home only too soon. And the returning visitors invariably say the same thing: 'Kyoto was full of tourists!'. In other words, people like themselves.

Onsen

With its volcanic geography, Japan has many hot springs where the groundwater, warmed by geothermal heat, emerges to the surface. With their warmth and mineral content, hot springs have long been valued for their therapeutic benefits, and resort facilities, from simple bed-and-breakfasts to full scale entertainment developments, have flourished around each of them. They are known as *onsen* (温泉), which simply means 'hot springs'.

Onsen as a term is defined by law. In 1948, the *onsenhou*, or Hot Spring Law, was enacted for the protection of hot springs and their safe usage (the prevention of natural gas explosions is a big issue). For a hot spring to be officially recognised, the water must be above a certain temperature at the source, and it must contain minerals or other matter above a certain level.

There are more than 3,000 *onsen* with accommodation facilities throughout Japan, from the northern tip of Hokkaido to the southern islands of Okinawa. Some are better known than others, perhaps for their geographical proximity to traditional centres of population. Arima *Onsen* (有馬温泉) near Kobe is one of the oldest recorded. It has undoubtedly benefitted from being close to Kyoto and Osaka (although it is also known for the therapeutic value of its water). Similarly, *onsen* around the Hakone (箱根) area in Kanagawa prefecture became well-known due to the proximity to Edo (later Tokyo), and for being on the roadside of the Tōkaidō route between Edo and Kyoto.

Other *onsen* are known for their therapeutic values. Kusatsu *Onsen* (草津温泉) in Gunma prefecture is deep in the mountains and hard to get to. Nevertheless, it has been one of the most popular and famous resorts for centuries, as its hot water, rich in sulphur, was believed to cure or at least ease the symptoms of diseases including syphilis and leprosy.

You didn't have to be sick to enjoy *onsen*, of course. They have been popular tourist destinations ever since tourism took off in the 19th century, and continue to attract weekend travellers.

Mainstream and modern (post-war) *onsen* accommodation has largely been in the form of indifferent business hotel-type affairs, with massive function rooms for corporate clients to entertain either their own employees or clients. Lately, guests are becoming more discerning, and the individual aesthetics of hotel owners are coming to the fore in relation to architecture, interior design and service style. Food is also becoming more important, with some high-end *onsen* offering auberge-style gastronomic experiences produced by skilled chefs working with local ingredients.

Volcanoes and earthquakes are annoying facts of life in Japan. Under the circumstances, *onsen* are some of the best compensation that nature could have given the Japanese people. We can stop being afraid or worrying about the earth moving under our feet as we enjoy a good soak in hot water from the earth's natural boiler room.

Take Me Out to the Snowland

In 1987, a run-of-the-mill romantic comedy film about a young couple played out against the backdrop of ski resorts was released. That film, *Take Me Out to the Snowland* (私をスキーに連れてって), went on to become a monster hit.

In the late 80s, Japan was riding high on the heady wave of the bubble economy. The younger generation had cash in their hands, but few ideas about how to spend it. Skiing was becoming popular, but the film pushed it into the mainstream and everybody started to flock to the pistes.

While poor resort infrastructure and chronic underinvestment saw queues at the chairlifts and waiting times of an hour or more, it was nevertheless 'cool' for young Japanese to be seen to be skiing. The well-known Prince Hotels group was one of the major developers of Japan's ski resorts, and still operates many of them today.

However, as the economy bubble burst, skiing holidays were among the first of the luxuries that one could do without in times of austerity. In 1993, there were about 18 million skiers in Japan. By 2013, that was down to around 8 million. There was another blow when the Seibu Group, owner of Prince Hotels, was hit by a serious fraud scandal. Many ski resorts shrank in size or simply closed down. Others reverted back to being the quiet hot-spring villages with modest bed and breakfast accommodation that they used to be.

As the Chinese economy started to roar, those who had made money from the Japanese skiing boom in the 80s and 90s pinned their hopes on their large neighbour, confident that they were on the up again. The Chinese skiing boom wasn't as universal as they might have hoped, but a sizeable number of the newly minted wealthy took up the sport, preferring to go to Japan for their new hobby.

Japan is currently going through its second ski boom, but it is very different from the first. The big difference is what the Japanese tourism industry calls 'the inbounds' – Australians and Chinese who come to enjoy 'Japow', also known as Japanese powder snow. They are seeking top-class resort infrastructure to match their high expectations, not the one hour-plus waiting times of yore. The early adapters to their demands, such as Niseko (ニセコ町) in Hokkaido, or Nozawaonsen (野沢温泉) and Hakuba (白馬村) in Nagano, are emerging as the winner, while others are still dreaming of past glories when it was enough for the skiers just to be standing on a crowded slope. For those people, it has never been so much about skiing. It is the yearning for the past when they were young, like the actors in the film.

日本の生き方

Decline of Sunday drivers and rise of Hell's middle-aged Angels

As of September 2017, there are about 81 million cars on the Japanese roads, of which around 61 million are privately-owned passenger cars.

Contrary to some news reports, the demise of the conventional car industry is very much premature and exaggerated. Despite population decline and the plateauing of the economy, car ownership has been steadily increasing in Japan.

Nevertheless, there is room for doomsayers in the Japanese automotive industry. For one thing, enthusiasm has gone, especially in younger generations. Among twentysomethings, the number of those who have expressed an interest in cars has declined by nearly 30 percent between 2001 and 2011. The decline is steeper among men than women.

There are many 'experts' offering various explanations for this trend. Some argue that the cost of car ownership is too onerous at a time of economic hardship. Others argue that cars these days are not as interesting as in the past. I am sure that the 'experts' have valid points, but they tend to approach the issue from a manufacturer's viewpoint, merely amplifying the talking points for industry lobbyists. The truth seems to be that consumers have simply changed their priorities – it is neither essential nor cool to own a car in modern Japan.

While car manufacturers fret about impending doom, imagined or otherwise, the motorbike industry has been there, done that and got the T-shirts to prove it. In 1980, over 6 million motorbikes were made in Japan. In 2016, that number is about 560,000. Nevertheless, motorbike manufacturers talk of a 'boom'. Although young people are staying away from the so-called 'suicide machines', older people seem to be flocking back to the two-wheelers. So much so, in fact, that the average age of a motorbike rider is said to be over 50. Motorbikes offer a cheaper outlet for those suffering a mid-life crisis than a Porsche or a Ferrari, and Harley Davidson machines have cornered nearly one third of the market. Unfortunately, the flipside of the rise in the silver-haired, born-again wild riders is that fatalities among the older riders are on the increase.

Motorbikes may be pointing the way ahead for cars. In the future, people will be choosing their mode of transport not through necessity or availability, but through preference and lifestyle.

Fishing

Fishing is a big deal in Japan. There are some 7 million anglers, and the pastime has a long tradition. During the Edo period, a feudal lord in present-day Yamagata prefecture encouraged samurai to master the art of fishing, maintaining that catching wild food would be a valuable skill in wartime. As urbanisation gathered pace, and the population started to be concentrated in big cities such as Tokyo and Osaka, fishing became a hobby for city dwellers, bringing them into the great outdoors.

In the 60s and 70s, catching fish was the paramount purpose of fishing. If this strikes you as rather obvious, you are obviously not a fishing type. While anglers competed to catch more fish, rivers and coastal waters suffered a decline in stocks. To sustain fragile rural economies dependent on anglers, local governments, as well as fishery and leisure industry groups, started to replenish stocks by releasing farmed fish into the water, especially in freshwater fishing areas. Some anglers also secretly introduced foreign species, such as bluegill and black bass, which are prized for their strength. These short-term, short-sighted interventions had serious negative effects on the ecosystem. Ultimately, if slowly, the environmental impact was recognised, and fishing manners expected of 21st-century anglers were adopted. Nowadays, catch-and-release is the norm.

Japanese fishing is perhaps notable for its variety of methods. While the size of catch still matters, the fishing method of choice is a matter of pride for an angler. The harder a method used to catch fish, the more respect an angler commands.

Tenkara fly-fishing (テンカラ), where a fly is attached to a fixed length of line, is a popular Japanese way of angling. Lure fishing, where casting does not require a wide and open space, is also popular, and there are always lively discussions as to the types of lures to be used for particular fish and fishing points. More exotic Japanese fishing methods include ayu (アユ) fishing, where a live sweetfish is used as bait. Sweetfish are very territorial, so if one sees another in its territory, the sweetfish attacks and is then caught by the hook that is attached to the live bait. The skills of navigating the sweetfish underwater take years to master, and competition among these anglers is fierce.

Perhaps the most unique Japanese method is *tanago* fishing (タナゴ釣り). A *tanago* is a type of carp that only grows to about 6–10cm and lives in rice paddies and their irrigation systems. To fish them, you use a miniature rod and tackle with a minute hook. Aficionados claim that using small gear with delicate skills to catch a tiny fish is proportionally equal to catching a whale using a large harpoon in terms of excitement. It is, of course, all in the mind of the angler. Like seeing a lush forest in a bonsai tree, it is almost Zen-like.

People of the mountains

Japan is 70 percent mountain, so it's no surprise that the sustenance from the bounty provided by mountains and the endless temperate rainforest that covered large areas was vital for indigenous peoples such as the *Jōmon* (縄文人), whose period lasted for some 14,000 years. Game, such as wild boar and deer, and plenty of fruits and nuts from the trees.

The mountain people eventually retreated eastwards and northwards, where the climate and geography made rice-growing more difficult, but some remained in the peaks. The mountains became a sanctuary, and a forbidden area for those who lived on the plains. Skip forward in time, and this forbiddance became associated with holiness. As the Japanese economy advanced, markets developed at the edge where the two worlds met: it needed the expertise of the mountain dwellers. All the magnificent wooden structures, those ancient temples or shrines we see around Japan, required the skills of expert woodcutters. Only they knew how to trek across the mountains to reach the desired trees, cut them down and carry them downstream for use on various building sites. They also made delicate woodcrafts, creating vases, bowls and other products which could be used on their own or become the basis for lacquerwares.

The ability of the mountain people to be able to crisscross seemingly impenetrable mountains and survive harsh conditions became a source of awe among the 'flatlanders'. As mountain people lived outside normal social hierarchy and structure, there were always elements of discrimination in their relationship with others. Nevertheless, people recognised the superhuman quality in those living up in the peaks, and this led to numerous folklore tales based on their mystery. There are numerous stories of *oni* (鬼), troll-like people who usually come down from the mountains or from hidden conclaves deep in the mountains to play mischief among the farmers. The word *oni* is believed to have derived from the term for 'big men'.

With the introduction of Western civilisation and the industrialisation of Japan from the mid-19th century, the number of mountain people, known as *sanka* (山窩), had dwindled. Urbanisation and the availability of work in the city lured them away from the mountains. The post-war economic recovery and mechanisation of the forestry industry finally lured the last of the mountain people out of their ancestral habitat and into the cities.

However, there are still those who believe in the mountain people living in pockets hidden deep in the Japanese mountains, and their legacy lives on through the rich tradition of woodcrafts they created.

日本の生き方

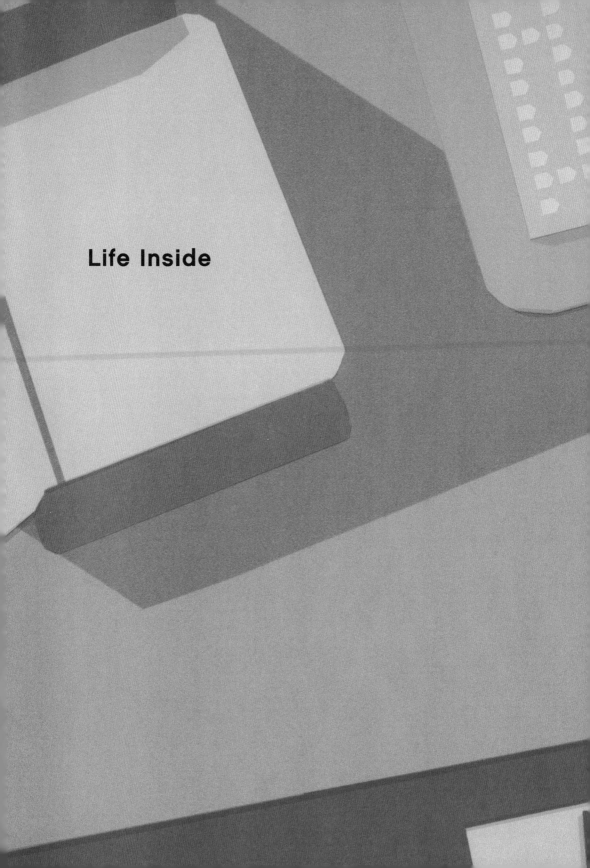

Life Inside

Go: Japanese Wimbledon

Igo (囲碁), or simply *go* (碁), is a board game believed to have been invented in China more than 2,500 years ago. Two players take turns to place a 'stone' – either black or white – on an intersection on a 19 x 19 grid. Each intersection of the grid counts as a piece of territory, and both players compete to surround more territories with their stones. Stones may be captured if they are isolated and surrounded by the opponent.

The rules of *go* are simple, but the game is complex, and tactical as well as strategic. While IBM's Deep Blue computer beat grandmaster Garry Kasparov at chess in 1996, it took until 2015 for Google DeepMind's AlphaGo program to beat a human at *go*.

Go arrived in Japan around the 7th century, from China via Korea, and became popular amongst aristocrats. In the 14th and 15th centuries, it spread across class divides and professional players appeared. They were hired by the rich and powerful as teachers, and became members of their entourages. In the peacetime of the Edo period, the Tokugawa shogunate offered patronage to master players, and ordinary people started *go* clubs to compete and study the game's tactics.

Currently, Japan has about 2.5 million *go* players and worldwide, there are about 40 million. Japan had the advantage of professionalising *go* earlier than other countries, so it dominated championship titles during most of the 20th century. Since the late 1980s, international tournaments such as the LG Cup and the Asian TV Cup have been held mostly in East Asia. After a short spell of Japanese dominance, Chinese and Korean masters have become dominant.

In reality, *go* has become international game in which the 'Big Three' of Japan, China and Korea are locked in a continuous battle for top place. I believe it is a healthy thing. We celebrate our common heritage and the mutual recognition of excellence in the players representing each nation. It is some common ground among often bickering nations, upon which we can gather together in a peaceful, contemplative game.

日本の生き方

Shōgi: Japanese chess

Like any other variation of chess worldwide, Japan's *shōgi* (将棋) is believed to go all the way back to India's ancient game of *chaturanga*. That game became *xiangqi* in China and *janggi* in Korea.

It is not clear when these variations of chess arrived in Japan, but it is believed to have been around the same time as the game *go*. The chess-type games would have differed in complexity, as any form of chess involves complicated rules with different types of playing pieces. Those earlier versions featured exotic (for the Japanese) pieces such as elephants and tigers.

By the 17th century, the game had simplified itself, become uniform, had rules, and developed into something similar to the present-day game of *shōgi*. At the same time, the concept of *mochigoma* (持ち駒) was incorporated into the game. Under this uniquely Japanese rule, a piece captured from an opponent can be reused by the opposite player and deployed at any time, and on any spot, on the board. This adds another level of complexity to the game.

Like *go*, *shōgi* enjoyed patronage from the Tokugawa shogunate and became popular across all classes. The Meiji Reformation also meant that both games lost such patronage. In 1924, professional *shōgi* players organised themselves into what was to become the Japan *Shōgi* Association.

Unlike *go*, *shōgi* is unique to Japan, and there is little interaction with overseas players. Nevertheless, *shōgi* has about five million players, more than *go* in Japan. While *go* is, at first sight, geometrically mysterious and wears an air of complexity, *shōgi* has direct visual appeal and the game is more combative. There are many tales of famous matches between master players of old, as well as new. There have been popular songs, TV dramas, films and even manga comic book stories written about *shōgi* players, ensuring more fans and a continued supply of future master players.

Martial arts

'Confucius didn't talk about occult, violent, obscene and spiritual matters.'

This saying, referring to the Chinese philosopher, was taken as a command against, or at least a frowning upon, engaging in any physical pursuits. The Boxer Rebellion against foreign powers in China at the turn of the 20th century failed in part because the 'boxers' (the Western term for practitioners of martial arts) were generally regarded as organised crime gangsters by the Chinese elite, who were invariably educated in accordance with Confucian teaching.

Being from what the Chinese considered a barbaric peripheral land, the Japanese did not follow the Old Master's example. Besides, during most of its recent history, Japan was ruled by those whom Confucius had warned of most: the martial class of samurai. That said, martial arts did not take off in Japan until the peace of the Tokugawa shogunate around 300 years ago. Before that, people did not practise martial arts – real life provided ample opportunity for those willing to try their martial prowess with inevitably fatal consequences for some.

During the Tokugawa shogunate, samurai became hereditary civil servants whose job was to carry out civil administrative work for the shogun or their feudal lords. Nevertheless, samurai had to maintain the semblance of being a warrior breed to maintain their social status. Various schools of swordsmanship (*kendō* 剣道 – 'the way of the sword') evolved. Skilled practitioners found gainful employment as sword masters throughout Japan.

Kendo became even more popular with the invention of the *shinai* (竹刀), a practice sword made from torn bamboo tied together. Previously, *kendo* was practised with a wooden sword, which meant it was a lethal blunt weapon. Fighting with one, even for training purposes, was a dangerous affair. A *shinai*, on the other hand, was softer, and allowed participants to engage in mock fighting quite safely. It also introduced the element of sport and competition to *kendo*.

Judo (柔道) was established by Jigorō Kanō (嘉納治五郎 1860–1938). He came from a wealthy merchant family in the Kobe area which was known for shipping and making *sake*. *Jujutsu* (柔術), the martial art of close combat without weapons, had been practised as part of wider martial arts, but Kanō gave it a structure, rules of competition, and made it into a sport that is practiced all over the world.

Karate (空手) literally means 'empty hand'. It actually originates from the school of Chinese martial arts like *kung fu*, and developed in Okinawa. It was introduced to mainland Japan at the turn of the 20th century and quickly became popular.

Thanks to the Japanese martial tradition and the respect with which people held the mastery of these arts and sport in general, martial artists enjoyed fame and a decent living. The tradition extends to modern-day variants of martial arts, such as Ultimate Fighting. Participants are generally respected by fans in Japan, who see them as masters rather than entertainers. You can find dōjō (道場), or gyms, for *kendo, judo* and *karate* in every corner of Japan.

Unfortunately for the Chinese, it took Bruce Lee to turn them away from Confucius' prejudices, which he did by beating the living daylights out of Japanese martial artists in his 1972 film *Fist of Fury*. Despite that, the Japanese love and respect Bruce Lee. That is because he was a master martial artist.

From Nintendo to Final Fantasy

Nintendo, the international games console manufacturer, began in Kyoto in 1889 as a printer of playing cards. Everything changed in 1983 when the company started to sell a *Family Computer*, shortened to *FamiCom*. A couple of years later, the rest of the world got the chance to buy the same console, now called the *Nintendo Entertainment System*, or *NES*. Nintendo went on to sell nearly 62 million of them.

It quickly dawned on Nintendo and other manufacturers that good software would increase sales. All of a sudden, manufacturers had to get creative.

Nintendo scored the first point against rivals Sony with the 1983 game *Mario Bros.* (マリオブラザーズ). Mario and Luigi started life as characters in the famous arcade game *Donkey Kong*, but nobody could have imagined that these two moustachioed Italian-American plumber siblings created by the Japanese men would be a worldwide hit. Having two hit characters was not enough, of course: they had to have amazing adventures to sell the game, the more adventurous the better. Nintendo's developers became storytellers as well, and debuted the *Super Mario Bros.* series of games in 1985, in which Mario and (if you're Player 2) Luigi go on various adventures. The idea of adventure soon evolved into role-playing with *The Legend of Zelda* (ゼルダの伝説シリーズ) in 1986. The *Super Mario* series has sold over 500 million copies to date, while *Zelda* hit the 80 million mark in 2017.

Nintendo was lucky in that it had its own captive characters in Mario and his entourage, rather like Disney's Mickey Mouse and friends. However, specialised game software companies sprung up to create games which were sophisticated both in terms of design and story. Major examples included the *Dragon Quest* series that first appeared in 1986, and the *Final Fantasy* games that began in 1987.

As sales of games consoles increased, the effect of the games had a huge impact on society. Almost every household had a console. As children got older, they went on to play time-consuming role-play games. The game titles became the way of making friends at school. The choice was no longer between girls or games, but which game over another. I use the word 'girl' deliberately, because the majority of gamers were boys at that stage.

More recently, however, the games boom seems to have lost some of its momentum. After about three decades of frenzied activity, the novelty is finally wearing thin. Consoles have become a part of the furniture. A little extra smoothness in Mario's movements doesn't impress much. When viewed in context, it seems that children's natural sense of balance has made them wise up, and they feel uneasy about devoting so much time to consoles. You could waste so much time playing one of those things and miss out on... this YouTube thing.

日本の生き方

From Kurosawa to Studio Ghibli

The biggest tragedy to befall Japanese cinema was the Second World War. When film as an art form was reaching its zenith globally, Japanese film was appropriated by warmongers as a propaganda tool. This loss of creative freedom asphyxiated Japanese film-making.

After the war, film was the king of popular entertainment. So many were made, but few have survived the test of time. *Seven Samurai* (七人の侍), the masterpiece of director Akira Kurosawa (黒澤明 1910–1998), and the calling card for Japanese cinema, was one of about 50 Japanese films released in 1954.

One thing that strikes the Japanese about *Seven Samurai* and most of Kurosawa's other films is how 'Western' they appear. In the hands of another director, there would have been more background details given to the story in terms of the place, time and backstories for each samurai. Consequently, the film is more universal in its appeal. However, it makes us a little uneasy that the story is not anchored to any geographical or historical facts that we Japanese are familiar with, and the film has a blunt feel about it. In that sense, Kurosawa's dramaturgy breaks from Japanese tradition and sensibilities. He also made samurai films inspired by Shakespeare's *Macbeth* (*Throne of Blood*) and *King Lear* (*Ran*), and made the Ed McBain detective novel *King's Ransom* into *High and Low*. Kurosawa's hero was the American director John Ford.

日
本
の
生
き
方

More in keeping with Japanese tastes are the films of Yasujirō Ozu (小津安二郎 1903–1963), known mainly for *Tokyo Story* (which came out a year before *Seven Samurai*). Nothing much happens in Ozu's films in terms of action. His stories are observations of ordinary people's everyday lives. Even Ozu's famous technique of shooting from a low angle makes the viewer feel as if we are witnessing events as we sit on the floor together with the actors. It makes us feel at home.

Unfortunately, before Kurosawa, Ozu or any other film-makers could properly restart Japan's film industry, it went into decline. People stayed at home and watched television. In the meantime, little happened in Japanese film, and those gems from the 1950s, in that brief golden era of Japanese film, remained like a time capsule, making them seem even more 'foreign' to us.

Japanese film came back onto the world stage with the animated films of Studio Ghibli in the 1990s. However, most of the studio's stories do not take place in Japan. Even the Oscar-winning *Spirited Away* (千と千尋の神隠し), while starting in an ordinary Japanese landscape, soon takes the viewer into a fantasy world.

While we have had some good Japanese films recently, it feels strange to see Japan through a film lens and on the screen. It may be that we are still struggling to fill the gap left behind by the unfortunate break in our film-making tradition during the war years.

Classical music

There is something about classical music that appeals to class-conscious people. One wonders what percentage of the audience at an opera performance chose to be there for the love of the music alone, and how many for the prestige.

From the start, classical music attracted the Japanese for its classy appeal. Japan had a somewhat limited cultural heritage when it came to music, and the sight of all the musicians dressed up to the nines in their white ties and tails with their glittering instruments struck us as incredibly sophisticated.

The Japanese started make pianos as soon as the country opened its doors to Western culture in the mid-19th century, but they only became affordable and popular among ordinary Japanese after the war. By then, piano makers had exhausted demands from schools for their instruments, and started to target ordinary households as their next market. As the economy went through its upward swing and household incomes increased, an upright piano became a key luxury item for those keeping up appearances.

Once you become an owner of a piano, it is advisable to be able to play it – and so the children of these middle-class households were sent off for piano lessons.

I suspect all the classical music prodigies from developing countries, Japan and Korea in the recent past, and China nowadays, are created in this manner. It may be the most non-threatening manifestation of a nation's middle-class one-upmanship.

I was signed up for piano lessons in my early teens to make some use of the piano my grandparents had bought for my aunt a long time before. I did not become a Japanese Mozart or Lang Lang – far from it. However, despite my lack of enthusiasm for the lessons, it did not bar me from appreciating classical music. At that time, there was a music critic in Japan doing to classical music what the American wine critic Robert M. Parker Jr. did to wine, cataloguing all the major recordings and giving them his purely arbitrary ratings. As a teenager, I fear I fell badly for this commercial snobbism and started collecting records in accordance with the critic's advice. Soon, I had a fairly respectable collection of Deutsche Grammophon's *Yellow Label* records at home.

Classical music in Japan has graduated from those days of snobbery and now enjoys a steady and more discerning audience. Tokyo alone has about 30 orchestras of note, of various sizes and reputations. We still have some peculiar traits left behind from the past: one of them being our fascination with Beethoven's Symphony No. 9, with its rousing choral finish. It has become a tradition that every major orchestra plays the deaf master's opus at the year-end concert. It is said that this has come about not out of any particular respect for the European Union and its anthem, but because it is a piece where both orchestra and choir members get paid for their performance – which has served as a nice bonus for musicians.

Japanese jazz

With the end of the Second World War came the Americans. With them came their barracks, and soldiers needed recreation and entertainment – both wholesome and illicit. Somewhat near the early end of that scale was music. Luckily, all the former musicians from the now disbanded Japanese military bands were looking for gainful employment. They were quickly marshalled to relatively lucrative engagements at the 'clubs' for those American barracks, where they learned to play a new kind of music called 'jazz'.

The military clubs were off limits to ordinary Japanese people, except for the musicians. However, that didn't stop the music seeping out of the clubs and finding its way into Japanese homes. Reconstruction work gathered pace to the sound of jazz and its syncopated and swinging rhythms. In those days, Western popular music was all called 'jazz' in Japan.

While the American military took the lead in beginning desegregation after the Korean War, American society was heading for the turmoil of the civil rights movement in the sixties. Around this period, the musician Art Blakey was making decidedly 'black' jazz with his band, the Jazz Messengers, which the critics called 'hard bop'. Blakey's music reached Japan via France, where it was featured in their *New Wave* films, and became huge hits – particularly his classic, *Moanin'*. Hearing of his popularity in Japan, Blakey toured the country with his band for the first time in 1960.

Upon arrival, Blakey was surrounded by enthusiastic fans. He was asked by one if he could be in a photo with him. 'But I'm black,' said the star. The fan replied, 'But, of course!'. Blakey instantly fell in love with Japan, and toured with the Jazz Messengers almost every year until his death in 1990.

Jazz is not the most popular form of music in Japan these days, but it still has a strong and faithful following. When the popularity of jazz was on the wane in the US, Japanese fans and record labels provided American musicians with steady support. Japanese jazz musicians are also thriving, and there are live jazz houses in every major city.

Jazz was perhaps the best gift that the American occupation brought to Japan in the turmoil of the post-war period.

Hikikomori

Since the 1990s, it has come to Japan's attention that there are a number of young people, mostly male, who refuse to interact with society. The issue was first raised when it was discovered that there were many students, mostly male, who refused to attend school. As time went on, their number swelled, and their average age increased.

According to statistics published in 2005, there were about 1.6 million people in Japan suffering from such social withdrawal. If you include those still managing to keep only minimum contact with the outside world, that number increased to more than 3 million people.

The word given to such people is *hikikomori* (引きこもり), meaning 'social withdrawal or isolation'. It applies roughly to those who refuse contact with society for more than six months or are diagnosed with various types of mental disorders affecting anxiety or adjustment, and so on. These conditions tend to manifest themselves in teenage years.

When the BBC picked up this topic for a report in the 2000s, it attracted a sizeable response from British viewers who recognised similar symptoms in themselves or family members. Such mental disorders and their manifestation in a hermit-like lifestyle are not specific to modern Japanese society, but they cannot be isolated from the society in which they occur, because social intercourse is the core issue.

The homogeneity of Japanese society and its pressure to conform may make it difficult for those who feel 'left behind' to find a suitable place for themselves. The ready availability of a virtual society online also seems to encourage anti-social behaviour in the real world. Presence and personality are easier to manipulate on the internet than in the real world.

In the strongly community-orientated society of Japan, individuality is difficult to maintain, whether in the workplace, school or other social arena. Unease with these circumstances may lead to mental disorders and agoraphobia in more vulnerable people. Although the symptoms of *hikikomori* were first discovered among young boys, we are now increasingly aware of – and alarmed by – its spread to the middle-aged and elderly, again mostly male. With the collapse of the convention of lifelong employment in Japan's corporate world, middle-aged workers forced to contemplate a career change in, say, their forties, and having to adapt to a sudden adjustment in their work environment, can make them vulnerable to a sudden onset of withdrawal. Elderly people in rural areas that are experiencing a rapidly decreasing population are also facing a change in their social landscape and are at risk of withdrawal.

It is tempting to dismiss those suffering from social withdrawal as weak-minded dropouts. However, one must remember that a society that takes care of its weak is stronger as a unit for its compassion. For a community-orientated society such as Japan, we ignore those who suffer at our own peril.

Family Life and Life's Milestones

Birth, Japanese style

It is rare for a Japanese child to be born to an unmarried couple. The Organisation for Economic Co-operation and Development (OECD) found that in 2014, only about 2.3 percent of babies were born out of wedlock in Japan. In the US, the figure was 40.2 percent, and 47.6 percent in the UK. Only Korea surpassed Japan in this respect, with just 1.9 percent of births outside marriage.

Childbirth in Japan is a cross-generational affair. Pregnant women tend to return to their parents' home when they are close to their due date. This practice is called *satogaeri* (里帰り), literally meaning to 'return home'. Women usually register with the hospital nearest their parents' house, and according to a survey in 2005, just over half of deliveries take place in hospital facilities.

About 50 percent of the husbands now accompany their wives at the birth, a 2011 survey found. This number increases with younger couples. Doctors are encouraging fathers to be present, and their recommendations seem to be heeded. Nevertheless, the tradition of women being with their parents near their due dates seem to be taking something away from this advice. Making a last-minute appearance at the take-off is probably not quite what is meant by 'sharing the experience'.

New Japanese mothers and their babies tend to stay longer in hospital than their overseas counterparts. A week seems to be the usual maximum, whereas in the US, mothers are encouraged to stay only overnight after the birth. When our son was born in the UK, my wife and I were encouraged to leave the midwifery centre as soon as we were able to, and we were all back home the same day.

Japanese women tend to return to their parents' homes with their babies to recuperate, another tradition that comes from a time when a mother's health after the ordeal of childbirth was far from secure. The word *tokoage* (床上げ), literally meaning 'to tidy up the futon', now means that a mother is strong enough to return to her normal duties – as well as caring for the baby by herself.

These outdated traditions also extend to facilitating fathers to remain at work right up to the birth of their child, and return immediately afterwards. They are expected, as a matter of course, to be estranged from their wives and babies for a period.

A widely known statistic is that Japan's birth rate has remained below 2 (less than the replacement value for the parents) for nearly half a century, contributing to the decline in its population and resulting in a rapidly aging society. While the active support provided by maternal grandparents is a nice way of bringing families together, it somehow works to exclude active participation from a husband's parents. The Japanese government is

actively encouraging companies to adopt paid paternity leave, but social norms based on tradition and workplace pressures are preventing men from taking full advantage of this. By taking cross-generational support for granted, Japanese society is making it more difficult than necessary for women to have babies and enjoy motherhood by choice. It is estimated that about 20 percent of pregnancies end in an abortion as a parental choice, as opposed to a termination for health issues for either a woman or her foetus.

With the serious population downturn already underway, Japanese government and society are both keenly aware of the need to change their attitudes towards childbirth. The reality, however, is changing very slowly. Given that childbirth is increasingly becoming just a once-in-a-lifetime event for most young parents, they still look to their own parents for advice, with their values and norms from a bygone era. And there are more of them around than babies these days.

Naming a baby

Japanese names have changed a lot throughout history, and they continue to evolve.

In the early 9th century, the custom of having a 'true name', or *imina* (諱) – one which can be written in one or two Chinese characters – became the norm. However, these were rarely used. There was a belief that a person's true name is spiritually linked to them. Revealing one's true name, therefore, was believed to have the effect of surrendering an important piece of oneself. Lovers swore their commitment to each other by letting the other person know their true name. Samurai pledged their allegiance to their lords by submitting the true names of themselves and their clan members in a *myôbu* (名簿), literally meaning 'register'.

People were mainly known by nicknames, aliases, or professional positions. In the simplest type of nickname, boys were named and known by the order of their birth. A boy called Tarō (太郎) meant he was the first-born. Jirō (二郎 or 次郎) was the second-born. This went on to Saburō (三郎), Shirō (四郎) and Gorō (五郎): the third-, fourth- and fifth-born, respectively.

In 1870, the modernising Meiji Reformation government ordered that people had to use a combination of surname and only one given name for all official purposes. With the adoption of a family register system to record Japan's population, the prolific and various use of true names and nicknames had come to an end. However, some chose to register their true names, and others chose their nicknames.

To illustrate the confusion, let's look at the example of Katsu Kaishū (勝海舟 1823–1899), who was a statesman of the Tokugawa shogunate. His nickname was Rintarō (麟太郎). The 'taro' in that nickname indicates that he was the first-born to his parents, while *rin* (麟) is a Chinese mythical animal which is said to presage the reign of a wise ruler. He was also known by his official title of *Awa no kami* (安房守), the governor of Awa province. The title had become merely honorary by the time of the Tokugawa shogunate, and gave him nominal precedence in the emperor's court, even if it was of little practical value. Katsu also had his true name of Yoshikuni (義邦), but it was hardly used in accordance with the tradition. When the new government ordered the tidying-up of people's names, Katsu chose Yasuyoshi (安芳) as his official given name, which was a play on his official title of *Awa no kami* (you have to be familiar with Chinese characters to appreciate it). Historically, however, he is most well known as Kaishū, meaning 'ocean ship' – the 'art name' he gave himself for being the founding father of Japan's navy.

We gave our son the name of Rintarō, partially in homage to Katsu, and also in part because the Chinese *rin* is a nice touch for a boy who has a link to China on his mother's side. However, many of my Japanese friends feel that the name is a little anachronistic with *taro*, signifying his first-born status. Names with three Chinese characters are also not that in vogue. Some suggested that the Chinese character for *rin* (麟), with so many strokes, might pose difficulties for him later in life when he has to write his name at examinations. By the time the poor boy finishes writing his name, the rest of his class would be on question two, some said.

日本の生き方

Modern Japanese parents must rely on their own aesthetic in choosing names. The biggest factor is the choice of Chinese characters to be used in the name. Meiji Yasuda Life, a life insurance company, publishes a yearly survey of baby names. In 2017, it found that out of 8,300 samples for boys, there were 4,204 variations, while in 8,030 samples of girls names, there were 3,604 variations. With so many different names, there is no Japanese equivalent of 'Tom, Dick or Harry', or their female counterparts.

According to the survey, the most popular boys' names for 2017 were 悠真 (Yūma, Haruma or Yūshin), 悠人 (Yūto, Haruto or Haruhito) and 陽翔 (Haruto, Hinato, Akito, Haruhi or Hinata). For girls, they were 結菜 (Yuina, Yuna or Yuuna), 咲良 (Sakura or Sara) and 陽葵 (Himari, Hinata, Hina or Hiyori). As you can see, the various ways of reading Chinese characters creates further chaos. 陽, meaning 'sun', is popular for boys. 結, meaning 'tie', has become popular for girls, as the recent series of natural disasters have made people aware of the importance of people's ties to each other, both in families as well as in local communities.

The imagination and creativity of Japanese parents in naming their children seems yet to have reached any limits, and it will be a long time before we settle for any set patterns. One constant theme is that these names represent the parents' wishes for their children and the kind of society in which the children will grow up. On that level, we may be continuing the tradition of seeing spirituality in names.

Education, or how to beat the Japanese school system

Compared to East Asian countries like China and Korea, Japan was not fanatical about education in the past. In China (and in Korea, in a similar way), Confucius' teachings and the imperial examinations based on them have been the enshrined tradition for millennia. Power, fame and fortune were available to those who studied and memorised the philosopher's *Analects* and other classical works. In Japan, a semi-literate meathead could become a feudal lord by scoring a lucky kill on the battlefield. For the Japanese, learning was cherished, but not the be-all and end-all.

Nevertheless, the peace that ensued under the Tokugawa shogunate promoted commerce and encouraged the whole population to become literate. This was achieved by the prevalence of private tutors (often moonlighting Buddhist monks and out-of-service samurai) teaching local children at *terakoya* (寺子屋), little shacks in a temple. The basic subjects were *yomi-kaki-soroban* (読み書き算盤), or reading, writing and abacus (basic arithmetic).

All these private arrangements became industrialised with the Meiji Reformation. To have your children educated became a duty under the constitution, and is still a part of the new constitution of 1946. Moreover, education became competitive. With the demise of the feudal class system, people were free to choose their careers. A massive education boom began, fuelled by a bestselling book called *An Encouragement of Learning* (学問のすすめ) published in 1872 by scholar and educationalist Fukuzawa Yukichi (福澤諭吉), who is also the current Mr 10,000-yen note.

Today, competition to get into a good school can be fierce. At each level, there are entrance examinations. Paradoxically, the fierceness of competition is fanned by parents' wish to avoid such exams. The aforementioned Fukuzawa founded a private university, Keiō Gijuku Daigaku, which has affiliated primary schools. Once you are at a Keiō primary school, you don't need to take entrance exams to progress through Keiō's middle school, Keiō's high school and, ultimately, Keiō University. The same system applies to many private educational institutions. Consequently, high-minded competitive parents send their toddlers to cram schools to prepare them for the entrance exams for primary schools.

While competition for the best schools remains fierce, the Japanese educational system is also experiencing a shrinking young population. At the not-so-top-notch end of the scale, schools are struggling to fill their classrooms. Recently, many educational establishments at all levels have introduced a system where applicant students are selected for admission on the basis of their school records and other achievements, rather than *pro forma* entrance examinations.

Private institutions exist by way of an escape route from entrance exam hell, but there are those who do brave the public education course, some for pecuniary reasons.

日本の生き方

Mostly, they are underage gladiators of the entrance exams, who are so clued-up as to the way the exams are presented that they can almost read the minds of those who set the questions. Those who survive this tortuous road tend to look down on the private education route and go on to occupy the higher echelons of Japanese society. But they are also doomed forever to search for the right answers and the perfect test scores in a world where the right answers are not immediately obvious.

With many educational institutions facing existential threats from a decreasing student population, it is high time that Japan rethinks the values and systems of education.

How the Japanese fall in love

Love may be timeless and universal, but courtship follows fashion. The Japanese courtship style has varied over history and geography. As I have already mentioned, aristocrats in the Heian period led a polygamous lifestyle, in which men called on each of their wives and any children were brought up by their mothers. In the east of Japan, where samurai thrived, family was a tighter unit by necessity. With on-going neighbourly feuds and shifting alliances, men had no time for cruising around the countryside from one wife to another, like a bee pollinating flowers. There, monogamy was the norm and wives had more powerful agency in family affairs.

Romance has taken many forms in Japan, as it often does. However, with the sudden onset of modern society under the Meiji Reformation, the Japanese collectively experienced a sudden social upheaval which produced a disconnect in our tradition, and we had to grapple with the question of what should be the new norm for love and romance – which ultimately lead to the question of how a family should be formed in modern Japan. This goes some way to explaining the heaps of boring romantic novels that were written in the last 150 years or so in Japan, few of which have withstood the test of time. We have not yet had our Jane Austen or Brontë sisters.

In the late 80s, Japanese TV produced what is called *torendi dorama* (トレンディドラマ), or 'Trendy Dramas'. They were essentially romantic comedies set in Tokyo, and were wildly popular. Against the backdrop of big city life, where people are strangely lonely amongst all-engulfing crowds, the protagonists met their fated partners in seemingly unexpected ways. After overcoming run-of-the-mill difficulties (disapproving families, uncooperative friends, work demands), they lived happily ever after. They were banal in the extreme. Nevertheless, in a simple tale of boy-meets-girl, young viewers sought inspiration as well as affirmation of their own real love lives.

Japanese TV is still producing latter-day incarnations of the *torendi dorama*, but they are not commanding the popularity or influence they once enjoyed. It appears that single Japanese have finally come of age, and do not require a TV drama as reassurance. After all, you only have to meet one right person. There is no need for that special personal experience to conform to what is peddled as mass entertainment.

Romance and love affairs reject generalisation, but if I may risk criticism, the Japanese tend to resort to group dating as a starting point for relationships. *Gōkon* (合コン) is the term that describes the parties and night-outs where eligible men and women get together. Usually, a man and woman who are already friends agree to bring their friends together to introduce each other, with the tacit understanding that some of the encounters may lead to romance. The *gō in gōkon* comes from the word *gōdō* (合同), meaning together, while *kon* comes from the German word *Kompanie*, meaning company. In the sixties, people were not into *gōkon*, but *gōhai* (合ハイ), which stands for 'together' and 'hiking'. Theirs was a more wholesome time. I suppose that the popularity of *go-kon* goes on to prove that the Japanese are a communal species even in dating.

The setup of *go-kon* serves to reassure the participants that their background checks have been done by the network of mutual friends. Any romantic developments from it can be subject to friendly feedbacks. It is less a stranger-in-the-night situation but more like a sit-com episode.

The flip-side of it is that Tinder and other similar modern dating apps are not popular in Japan in the way they are in other western countries. Make no mistake, there are hordes of them in Japan, but they are used more in relation to the search for sexual partners, rather than romantic relationships. Chance encounters for the Japanese is sexy but not romantic. You need first to 'belong' to 'us' by being vouched for by a mutual friend to show that your intentions are proper and honourable.

Weddings and marriage

Fewer people are getting married in Japan, and those who do wed are getting older. The latest available statistics show that about 5 in 1,000 people married in 2016, as opposed to more than 6 in 1,000 in 1996. The average age for a bride is 31.1, while for a groom it is 33.3. Twenty years ago, they were 25.2 and 27.8 respectively.

Still, finding a mate is the biggest purpose of life for earthbound animals, including the Japanese, and marriage continues to be a life goal that many people are trying to achieve. It is just that society and modern lifestyles are making it somehow more difficult with added complications.

Japanese brains may be stressed from everyday life, but nature finds a way of bringing people together. About 25 percent of Japanese women getting married are pregnant, according to government statistics from 2010. In tropical Okinawa prefecture, the percentage goes up to more than 40 percent.

Pregnancy before marriage used to be frowned upon, but not so much now. With population decline a serious national issue, people have slowly become more benign towards a young couple with a little one soon to follow. Sadly, the same government statistics show that about 40 percent of such marriages end in divorce.

Marriage necessitates a wedding – a relatively recent custom in Japan. In the Heian period, aristocratic marriages were basically private coming-out parties for hitherto clandestine lovers. Between the 12th and 19th centuries, weddings among samurai families became more ornate, as the ceremony came to symbolise the alliance of two families. Customs such as an engagement ceremony, called a *yuinō* (結納), where the families of the bride and groom exchange gifts, developed gradually during this period, and were later copied by commoners. The actual wedding usually took place at the home of whichever family with whom the newlyweds were to live, and there was little religious tone to the ceremony.

Weddings as a celebration of a couple are a recent phenomenon. As such, modern Japanese people (well, mostly women) had a free hand in creating the new custom.

Weddings at a Shinto shrine became popular in 1900 after Emperor Taishō (大正天皇), then still a crown prince, married his wife in the Shinto shrine in the palace compound. This was the first time any religious organisation had been involved in people's matrimonial affairs in Japan.

Some modern Japanese brides-to-be aspired to a European style white wedding in a church due to their exposure to Western culture. However, Christian churches did not take kindly to the idea of letting non-believers use their facilities to satisfy young women's fancies. Many insisted on religious conversion before the ceremony. Sensing a gap in the market, Japanese hotels and other commercial function venues started building mock chapels to offer 'Christian-style' weddings, which became very popular.

Not to be outdone, Buddhist temples tried to cut in on the action, but suffered from image issues as they were too associated with death and funerals. Temples continue to promote themselves in this competitive field, but are yet to claim any significant share of the market.

In the end, the most popular trend nowadays seems to be what is called *jinzen-shiki* (人前式), or an 'in-front-of-people' wedding. Couples invite their friends and relatives to a party and exchange their vows in front of them.

Another nice Japanese wedding custom is *goshūgi* (ご祝儀). Instead of buying wedding gifts for the newlyweds, guests bring cash in a celebratory envelope and present it at the reception area before entering the party venue. The going market rate is about ¥30,000–50,000 per guest. This means that neither the newlyweds nor the bride's father have to pay for the wedding party. It is a self-financing affair.

In the course of a typical wedding party, the newlyweds change their outfits in a custom called *o ironaoshi* (お色直し). If they start the party with the bride dressed in a Western-style white wedding gown and the groom in a matching morning coat or similar (or both in the traditional Japanese ceremonial kimono), they may change into more casual dress at around halfway through the party. It is yet another recent tradition.

At the height of the Japanese bubble economy in the 1980s, professional wedding organisers came up with outrageous practices, such as newlyweds entering a party venue in a gondola suspended in mid-air with lots of dry ice smoke preceding their progress. Nowadays, such extravagance is shunned, or just laughed at. Still, the cake-cutting ceremony and candle-lighting (where newlyweds go to each table to greet the guests and light a candle on the table) are still popular.

All in all, the purpose of recent wedding receptions is for newlyweds to thank both sets of parents for their love and support up to the wedding. Usually, fathers of the bride *and* groom make a speech, and all the guests secretly hope for tears. Being Japanese, they are almost invariably unaccustomed to public speaking or shows of emotion.

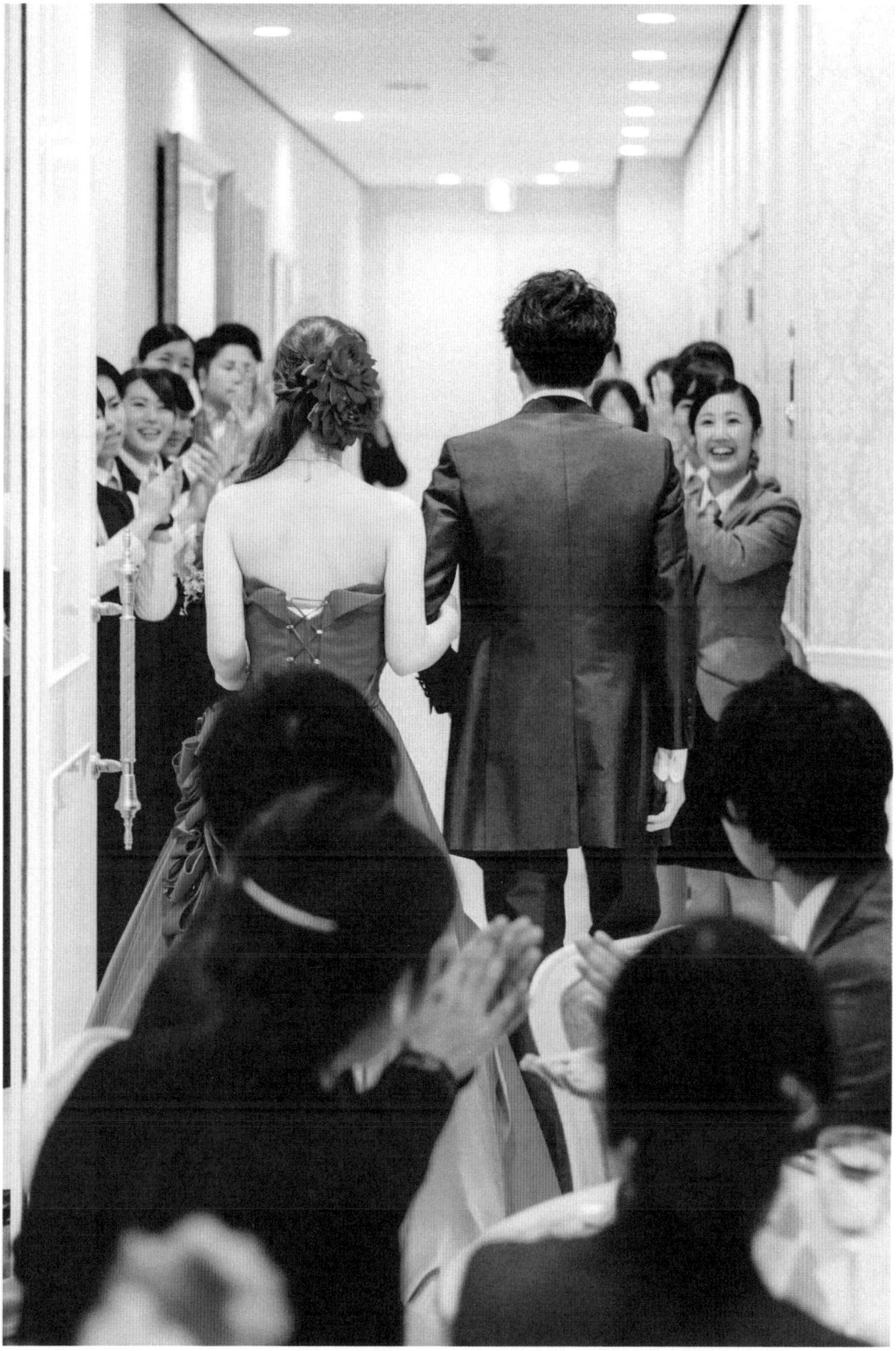

Bentō box wars

The oft-cited argument for a school uniform is that it ensures equality among children by eliminating the element of futile fashion contests. Somehow, the same argument may need to be applied to food in Japanese schools.

Most public elementary and junior high schools provide school lunches, called *kyūshoku* (給食). Often, children take turns to serve the food to their classmates, so they learn not only about food, but to take pride and joy in serving others, be grateful for the meal, and to enjoy communal eating.

Kyūshoku has eased the pressure on parents by removing the daily need to pack a lunchbox, or *bentō* (弁当). *Bentō* are only needed for such special occasions like school outings and picnics on school sports days, or *undōkai* (運動会).

To be sure, *bentō* is not just for school lunches. The word is used for any packed mobile meal. Adults enjoy *bentō* at, say, cherry-blossom viewing parties and other outings, and some famous restaurants are known for making *bentō* boxes fit for such occasions, with extravagant contents and aesthetically pleasing presentation.

Still, nobody expected the extravagance to hit *bentō* for school children. The most my generation enjoyed were wiener sausages sliced on one side to make them look like miniature octopuses with their tentacles.

Somehow, around the 2000s, people started making children's *bentō* boxes depicting popular cartoon characters, cars or animals, using ingredients to draw and create the images. They are called *kyaraben* (キャラ弁), a word created from 'character' (as in characters from animation films) and *bentō*.

The emergence of blogs and social media fanned the boom, with an ever-increasing number of creators uploading photos of their opuses online for all to see, appreciate, and emulate.

It is putting parents with less time on their hands (not to mention creativity or dexterity) under pressure in the never-ending battle for one-upmanship, but the boom shows no sign of abating. Probably because it is linked with that most Japanese of aesthetic values: *kawaii* (かわいい), or cuteness.

日本の生き方

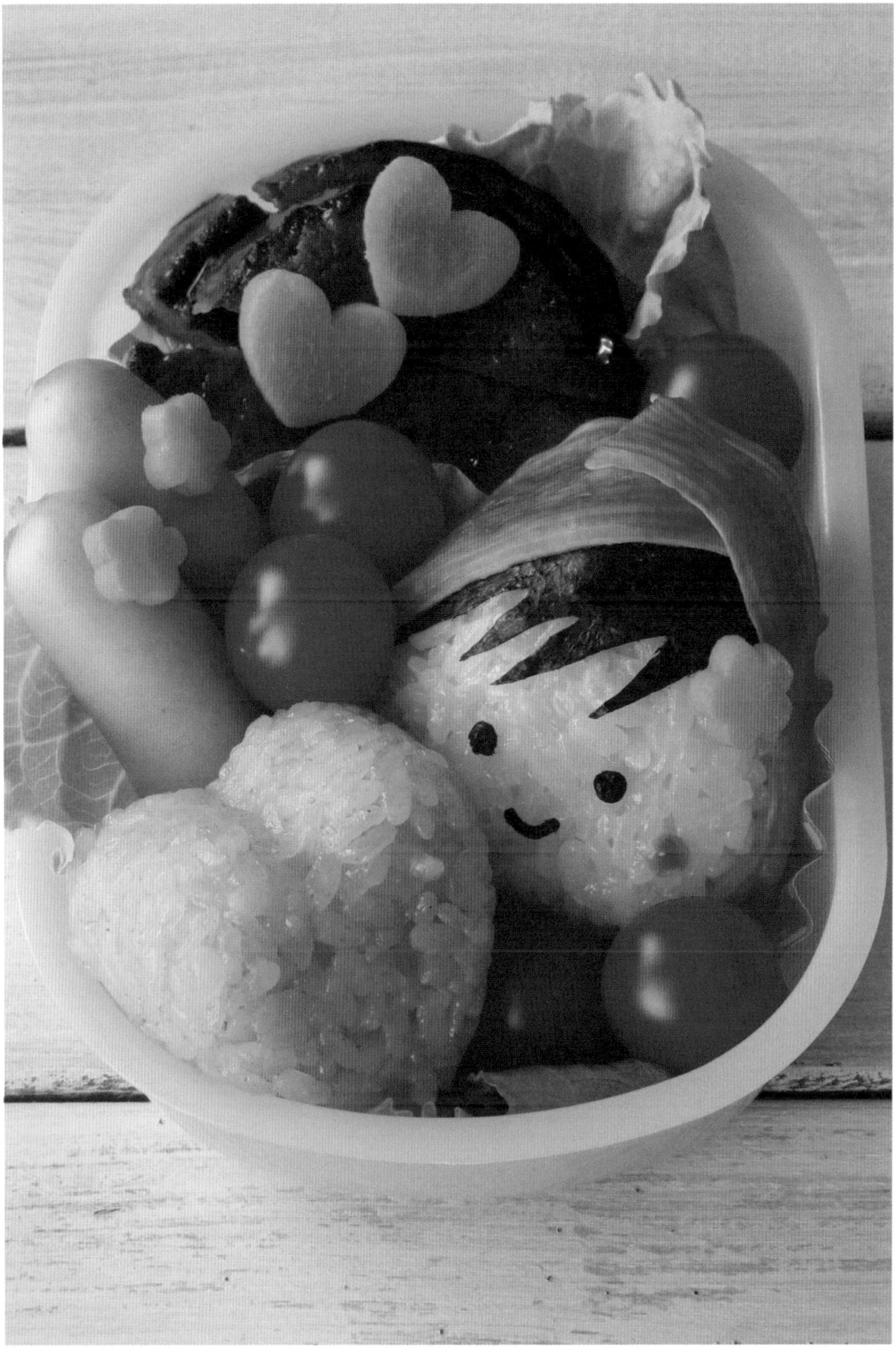

How to make a bentō box

1. **Think about the proportions.** Bentō boxes can be as elaborate as you want and may feature many items, but the three key ingredients are rice, fish or meat, and pickled vegetables. These are the foundation upon which any bentō box variations are built.

2. **Add flavour to your rice.** The main ingredient of any bentō box is rice. Unfortunately, rice does not hold its flavour particularly well when it gets cold. The easiest way to maintain cooked rice's delicate flavour is to add salt – which also acts as a preservative – or alternatively, try adding some sesame seeds. Other ways to improve the quality of your bentō box rice, include cooking it with other flavourful ingredients, such as bamboo shoots, diced octopus or clams.

3. **Keep your bentō balanced.** As part of a balanced diet, a bentō box should include a main source of protein. This can be fish, often grilled with salt (again, good for preservation), or meat cooked in such a way which keeps, such as roast beef. For a vegetarian bentō, you can try beans (edamame are good) or tofu as a protein source.

4. **Pickled vegetables** are usually inserted in a corner of the box, to complement the balanced diet, as well as to add colour and flavour. Sour and crunchy vegetables also help to satisfy the appetite.

5. **Think about appearance.** Remember that the aim with a bentō box is to create a meal that is as appealing to the eyes as to the taste buds. Colour is key to a visually exciting bentō box. Choose brightly coloured vegetables to contrast against the rice.

6. **Avoid excess liquid.** For ease of transporting, it is best to avoid watery foods or anything with a lot of sauce, as liquid may leak out. If you do want to include sauces or condiments, then use a separate container.

Divorce

One in three marriages ends in divorce in Japan. The number is not as bad as in the US or UK, where nearly half of all marriages end in divorce, but we are getting there.

People decide to go their separate ways for many different reasons, even in Japan. Nevertheless, the top three causes for divorce seem to be, in reverse order, money, infidelity and irreconcilable differences. I suppose the last one covers all manner of sins.

Most divorces occur in the first 15 years of marriage, but divorce amongst mature couples is also on the rise. Common horror stories often involve a workaholic husband who has had little time for his wife returning home one evening to find the house empty, with a note informing him that she could not stomach the prospect of retired life with such an uncaring husband suddenly at home all the time. The moral of the story is that handing over paycheques is never a substitute for love and affection.

One feature of Japanese divorce is that there is little pressure from the legal system to keep a marriage alive. In Christian countries, marriage used to be sacred, to varying degrees in each country, and divorce was difficult to obtain. Even with the advent of no-fault divorce, Western legal systems tend to impose a cooling-off period. There is no such last-minute lingering in Japan. If both parties are determined to go their separate ways, it only requires the submission of a form at the local government office to show their consent. Divorce is very unsentimental and keeps lawyers' involvement to a bare minimum, which is good news.

Japanese courts tend to get involved in divorce cases where children's custody is an issue. Uncommon in jurisdictions of developed countries, Japanese courts tend to look at a child's needs, as opposed to each parent's right to access. I believe there should always be room for the Japanese approach. Parents are paying for their lawyers, who will happily argue *ad nauseam* for their client's rights. Children's interests are often overlooked.

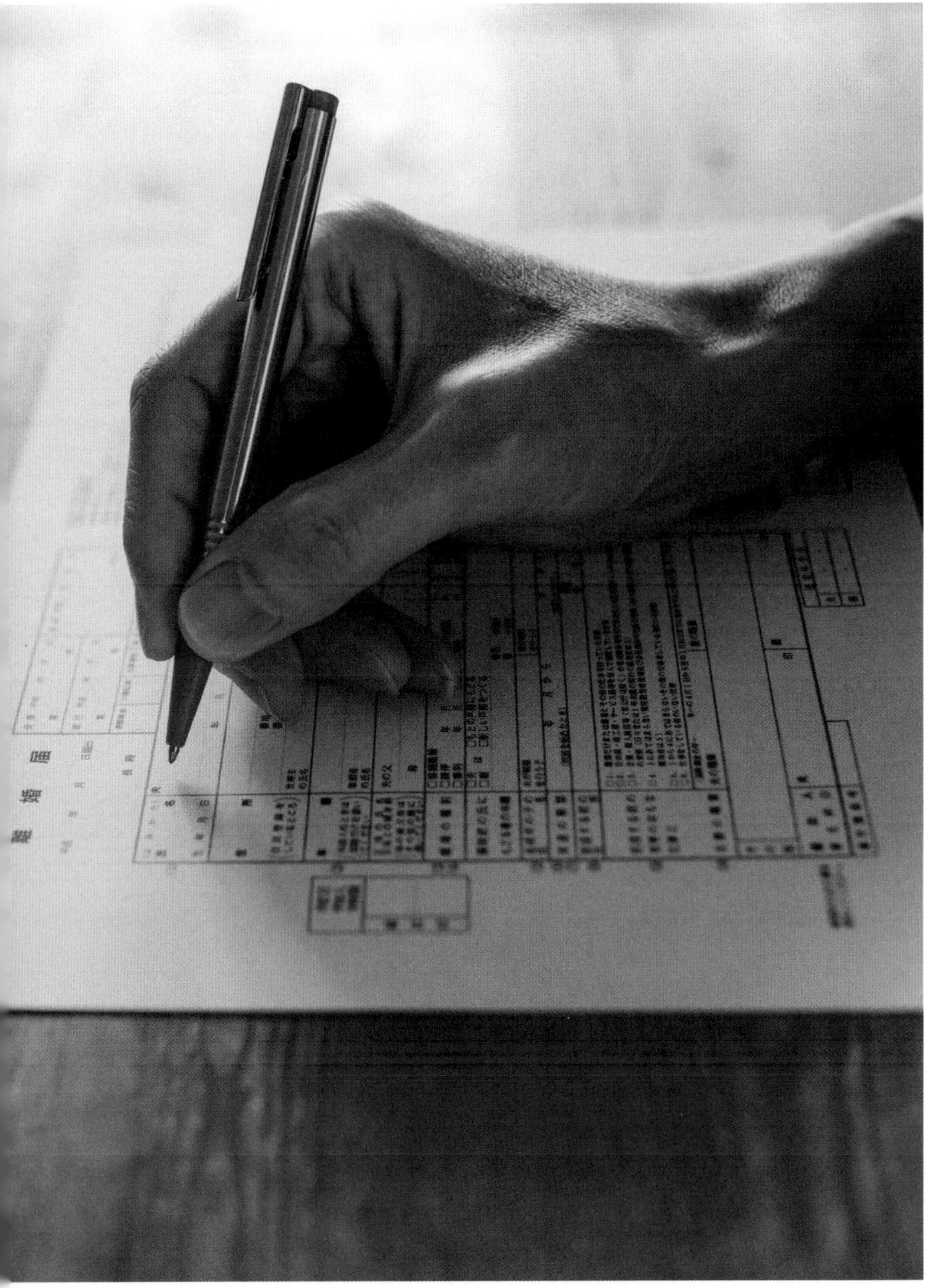

How to live to a hundred

While aging populations are a global phenomenon, Japan stands out from the crowd for its population's long life expectancy (about 84 years), the number of elderly (more than 33 million are over 65, about 26 percent of the Japanese population) and the speed at which the population is becoming aged (the number of the elderly has multiplied four times over the last 40 years). We are the triple-crown winner or the Helen Keller of the aging world, depending how you look at it.

The longevity of the Japanese, 86 for women and 80 for men, ranks second in the world to Hong Kong and is the envy of everywhere else. For the Japanese themselves, it is pleasing to be praised for what we achieve as a matter of habit, rather than as a result of strenuous effort.

The Japanese are sitting at a comfortable crossroads of both Western and Chinese medical traditions. We enjoy one of the best universal healthcare systems in line with what centuries of Western medical advances can provide. At the same time, the Japanese attitude towards health is deeply influenced by the Chinese thinking of yōjō (養生), or nurturing health through lifestyle. Attending to illness is the last resort.

The Japanese diet contributes hugely to the health of our nation in this respect. Nutritional balance has always been a part of our cuisine, even in the humblest of daily meals. Ichijūissai (一汁一菜) is the word to describe the most modest of meals, referring to one soup and one vegetable dish to go with a bowl of rice. A healthy appetite is praised as a product of hard labour, and gluttony is shunned as unseemly behaviour.

The weak links in an otherwise ideal diet are perhaps the reliance on rice and the use of too much salt. The Japanese are nevertheless aware of this. Metabo (メタボ), a Japanese–English term for metabolic deficiency, is currently a watchword for the health-conscious, and people are avoiding excess intake of carbohydrates. Faced with low demand for rice, producers are providing the market with healthier products such as zakkokumai (雑穀米), rice mixed with millet as an alternative to pure white rice. Too much salt seems to result in relatively high instances of stomach cancer among the Japanese; to go some way to combatting this, manufacturers are filling supermarket shelves with all sorts of products, from pickled vegetables to miso paste, labelled gen-en (減塩), or 'reduced salt'. The health food industry in Japan is happily led by health-conscious consumers.

日
本
の
生
き
方

Funerals

As a social display of decency for a deceased person's family, funerals are for the living. The death is, for all intents and purposes, just an excuse for the occasion. In Japan, death brings family together and reminds us of our Japanese-ness.

My mother regularly tells her children that she wants her ashes scattered in the sea when she passes away. Each time, we have to remind her that it is illegal to litter, especially a dead person's bones, and, first and foremost, we would have to do what seems decent in the eyes of those who know her.

At this juncture, I might have to make it clear that cremation is the norm in Japan, for hygiene reasons.

There is nothing like a funeral to encourage the building of consensus. Family members have to be notified to gather, even the estranged and feuding ones. There may be inevitable discord to follow over the inheritance, but procedures for a funeral ceremony must be agreed as a matter of urgency – usually within 24 hours of the deceased's passing. Again, due to hygiene issues.

It is easiest to build consensus on the socially accepted norm. Therefore, a local funeral service provider is contacted, as well as the temple where the family tomb stands. Any of the deceased's eccentric wishes, such as to disappear under the waves, would be first to go.

There is a wake before the day of funeral, called *otsuya* (お通夜). It literally means 'all night long'. In reality, it would just be a limited time (about two hours) in the evening, where people gather around the body, now properly cleaned and dressed by a professional, listen to a Buddhist monk reciting some mantra (while each family member belatedly wonders if a Buddhist ceremony was a no-no according to the deceased's wishes), then provide the guests with a light meal, usually *sushi*, which is quick to order and easy to share, plus *sake*. The chief mourner, or *moshu* (喪主 – usually the deceased's spouse or the eldest child), is busy dealing with the guests, thanking them for their attendance despite the short notice and/or long distance. Other family members are also busy, wondering if they have ordered enough *sushi* and *sake* to go around. Those closest to the deceased are all too busy putting on a show of decency and spare only a fleeting thought about what the deceased actually wanted for the funeral.

On the day of the funeral, most of the *dramatis personae* return for the more elaborate Buddhist funeral rituals, including the monk and the guests, and anyone who could not make the previous night. The deceased's family members are now resigned to the fact that the bones will be heading for the family tomb in the monk's temple, and that the new generation of family members will have to keep paying a maintenance fee for it. The *moshu* continues to be busy, exercising the superhuman diplomatic skill of displaying an adequate amount of sorrow while trying to remember the names and faces of the deceased's extended network of friends and contacts. One good thing is that they bring a packet of condolence money, called *kōden* (香典) – literally, in a wonderful Japanese euphemism, 'incense money'. Apparently, ¥5,000 per person is the going rate. This would go only so far in easing the cost of the funeral, not to mention the tomb fee for the temple, but every little helps.

Both the wake and funeral ceremony may be held at the deceased's home. If there are space issues, the funeral services can rent out their hall, or the family temple would oblige. In which case, the monk wouldn't have as far to travel.

After the ceremony, the coffin is moved to a specially made *reikyūsha* (霊柩車), or hearse, which is usually a black limousine with an elaborate Japanese roof design, to be carried to the local crematorium. Family members follow in separate cars.

Most crematoria in Japan are run by the local government, except in Tokyo, where a private company has a monopoly. It is usual for family members to watch the coffin going into the furnace. In Chinese and Korean traditions, rooted in Confucian teaching, family members are supposed to cry at this point, and they usually do so out loud. This is the first moment when family members are finally allowed some private moments with the deceased, away from the social spotlight which has shone on them ever since the death, and they cry.

The bones, whiter than you could ever imagine, come out of the furnace and all the family members are encouraged to pick them up with special chopsticks to put them into an urn. Finally, the crematorium attendant scoops the remaining bits and pieces into the urn, which is then sealed. You take the urn back home and make arrangements with the monk to put it in the family tomb at some future date.

Funerals have produced two major hit films. Director Jūzō Itami (伊丹 十三) released *Osōshiki* (お葬式 – *The Funeral*) in 1984, while Yōjirō Takita (滝田 洋二郎) won an Oscar for 2008's *Okuribito* (おくりびと – *Departures*). Both are highly recommended.

Some good news for my mother is that you are now legally allowed to scatter ashes, provided that they are properly ground into dust and the scattering is carried out with moderation and according to guidance from the Ministry of Justice. I'm still not that keen on the prospect of grinding my own mother's bones, though.

No sex, but perversion, please, we are Japanese

The Japanese have been a promiscuous lot since time immemorial. In the official Chinese chronicle of the 3rd century, it was noted that we were polygamous, regardless of social class. Many ancient Shinto festivals were basically orgies, and the devotional participants believed that these occasions were sanctioned by the gods, who were pleased with this licentious and healthy display of lust. There are even poems about those religious speed-dating events recorded in the oldest anthology of *waka* poetry, *Man'yōshū* (万葉集), from the 7th or 8th centuries. The art of seduction, and being seduced, was *de rigueur* for aristocrats of the Heian period, and the tradition continued even when they lost their political power to the samurai. Commoners were not left out, and the practice of *yobai* (夜這い) was prevalent throughout Japan. This involved young men calling on their sweethearts at night by sneaking into their bedchambers, avoiding detection by family members.

The sexual freedom of the Japanese in the past may have had something to do with the absence of religious taboo. Neither Shintoism nor Buddhism sought to impose limits on people's sexual behaviour (unless you were a strict-order Buddhist monk). The freedom extended to homosexuality. Same-sex love was not only tolerated, but was fashionable at certain points in Japanese history. Many warlords from the Age of the Warring States are known to have been homosexual or bisexual.

Japan's sexual culture is best manifested in the series of pornographic *ukiyo-e* woodblock prints which were very popular in the Edo period. Artists and woodblock-carving artisans competed to create the most intricate and robust masterpieces.

All this changed with the Meiji Reformation. In an effort to modernise Japan, society became prudish. The slogan from the era was 'wakon yōsai' (和魂洋才), or 'Japanese spirit with Western technology'. Clearly, the effect of Westernisation was not contained in the fields of science and technology, and crept into people's social mores.

In a rigid, hierarchical society, sexual freedom was a welcome, even necessary, outlet for people's desires. In an ostensibly free-for-all society, Japanese people became self-conscious, and society became strait-laced in accordance with the restrictive sexual mores imported from the West. Sexual promiscuity was frowned upon as irregular and deemed a blemish on that person's character.

This attitude continues today. Extra-marital affairs among celebrities are a staple of the media, and the culprits are socially condemned by those who cannot help themselves from being the first to throw stones with ugly, self-righteous mirth on their faces. Japanese society has become hypocritical.

At the same time, this over-suppressed sexuality is manifesting itself in the most unwelcome ways. Almost every day, someone is arrested for groping women on a crowded train. You cannot deactivate the shutter noise from the camera in iPhones

日
本
の
生
き
方

sold in Japan because there have been too many perverts using them to take 'upskirt' photos of unsuspecting women.

Apart from perversion of the criminal kind, we have a hypocritical legal framework regarding prostitution, whereby it is illegal, but there are no set penalties for either the sex worker or the customer. There has been no serious attempt at rationalising laws for nearly 60 years. Our pornography industry has global notoriety, but it is a far cry from the artistry of *ukiyo-e* paintings, and is usually misogynistic in tone.

Nearly 150 years have passed since the Meiji Reformation, but the Japanese appear unable to find balance in our sex lives.

Holidays and Celebrations

January: New Year's Day

Oshōgatsu (お正月) is hugely important in Japan. Frankly, we Japanese are baffled about why most of the West (with the notable exception of Scotland) ignores this most auspicious of days and treats it like a minor addition to Christmas.

While I'm discussing 'New Year's Day' here, *Oshōgatsu* actually refers to the whole month – although the holiday period extends to the first three days of January these days. The first seven days of the month are commonly referred to as *matsunouchi* (松の内), literally 'inside the pine', because we use evergreen pine twigs for decoration, and a certain levity is temporarily permitted in the workplace.

One of the most important rituals for New Year's Day is a visit to the local shrine to pray for the Shinto gods' blessings for the forthcoming year. This observance is called *hatsumōde* (初詣), or 'the first visit to the shrine of the year'. Stepping out into the crisp, cold winter air and joining the queue of others all exhaling white mist just adds to the sense of occasion. Some dress in their best kimonos, which adds colour to the spectacle.

Returning home, we eat a special meal called *osechi-ryōri* (御節料理), literally meaning 'the meal for a special occasion', but it invariably refers to New Year's Day. *Osechi-ryōri* is basically a bentō consisting of various foods with some connotation of good luck. Here's what a typical box contains:

黒豆 kuromame

Black soybeans boiled with sugar. They are believed to ward off evil spirits, and the word *mame* (bean) also means 'diligent'.

かずのこ kazunoko

Marinated herring roe for fertility and productivity.

田作り tazukuri

Baby sardines simmered nearly dry in soy sauce and sweet sake. *Tazukuri* translates as 'making rice paddies', and symbolises a good harvest.

紅白かまぼこ kōhaku kamaboko

Red and white fishcakes. Red is for warding off evil, and white is for purity.

栗金団 kurikinton

Chestnuts covered with golden cream usually made from sweet potato. Chestnuts, or *kachiguri* (かち栗) are associated with the verb *katsu* (勝つ), which means 'to win', and the golden colour for richness.

ぶりのやきもの buri no yakimono

Grilled amberjack. This fish has different names in Japanese as it grows, so it is eaten in the hope of development or promotion.

えびのやきもの ebi no yakimono

Grilled shrimp. Shrimp is a symbol of longevity because of its long antennae and curved shape – to symbolise remaining active even when your posture is bent.

紅白なます kōhaku namasu

Shredded radish and carrot marinated in vinegar. The red and white of the vegetables are for good luck.

昆布巻き kobumaki

Simmered sea kelp rolled with fish meat or burdock. Konbu (昆布), meaning 'kelp', is a pun on *yorokobu* (喜ぶ), or 'to rejoice'. The rolled shape refers to books, and this dish is for academic achievement.

八つ頭 yatsugashira

Simmered taro (or eddo) is for fertility, as root vegetables produce plenty of crops.

The above selection is just an example. *Osechi-ryōri* combinations differ by region, as well as family traditions and preferences. Most dishes take a lot of preparation, but keep well, so families spend the run-up to New Year's Day preparing *osechi* and spend the rest of the holiday not having to cook.

February: Valentine's Day (or how a chocolate company orchestrated a cultural coup)

February in Japan is notable for a bizarre celebration of recent fabrication: Valentine's Day (バレンタインデー).

The Japanese noted that Westerners attached romantic values to Valentine's Day. Taking a cue from this, certain enterprising Japanese businessmen in the confectionary industry started a PR campaign encouraging people to give loved ones some chocolate on Valentine's Day.

The first Valentine's campaign was started by Morozoff (モロゾフ), a Kobe confectionary business, in 1936 – although it was aimed at foreigners in Japan. After the war, Morozoff tried again, this time targeting Japanese consumers. By the late 50s and early 60s, Valentine's was all the rage.

Somehow, this giving of chocolates became a one-way affair. Social convention dictates that the chocolates should be given by women to men. Nobody knows why. If I were to hazard a guess, Japanese women, having been oppressed by social norms to be merely passive actors in the game of love, welcomed the opportunity to express their affection openly in the form of chocolate.

As for the men, Valentine's has become a bit of competition. Some men receive multiple chocolate gifts from their adoring female fans, while others receive nothing. This has created awkward situations in workplaces and schools. Hell hath no fury like a jealous Japanese man deprived of chocolate.

This custom has given way to the most Japanese of social conventions: *giri-choco* (義理チョコ), or 'duty choc', meaning that the gift of chocolate is given out of obligation to save the receiver's face, rather than as a token of affection. A lot of bosses are laden with face-saving chocolate from considerate female colleagues on 14th February. And it's not cheap, either. Recent estimates put the average spending at around US$45 per woman.

Statistics say that about 20 percent of annual chocolate sales occur on and around Valentine's Day, so this tradition is unlikely to melt away any time soon.

March: Girl's Day

Hinamatsuri (ひな祭り), or Girl's Day, is when we hope for and celebrate the healthy growth of girls in our families.

On 3rd March, we put out decorations and dolls depicting a scene from courtly life in the Heian period. The dolls of a prince and his consort are placed on the top of a decorative display, with their ladies-in-waiting and courtly musicians in the lower parts, together with elaborately made miniatures of furniture and ox-drawn carts, the transportation of choice for any self-respecting aristocrat of the time. Basically, it is playing house and creating scenes of the domestic bliss of elegant, well-to-do families of a bygone era.

As a boy, I had little interest in a celebration using dolls. My interests were mostly to do with the treats served on the occasion. There is amazake (甘酒), a sweet, mostly non-alcoholic sake, and sweet rice cakes called hishimochi (菱餅).

The popular myth is that the longer the display is left out past Girl's Day, the harder it will be for the girls of such households to get married. From playing house to this unwarranted pressure to marry from a very early age, I am not sure if this festival can withstand the scrutiny from modern-day political correctness. Still, you cannot take away the joy from the girls, who just want to have fun with the dolls or enjoy a beverage of dubious alcohol content.

May: Boy's Day

The day for celebrating boys and wishing for their healthy growth is on 5th May.

Unlike Girl's Day and its dolls, on Boy's Day we take out miniature armour, swords and arrows for display, representing a family's wish for their boys to grow up to be brave and strong. Yoroi kabuto (鎧兜) means armour, and boys' hearts soar at the sight of an awesome martial display. Parents have a tough time stopping their children from playing with the decorations. Inevitably, the miniature swords are the first to get damaged from too much mock fighting. This may explain why there are so many precious antique dolls from Girl's Day on the Japanese version of the Antiques Roadshow, but very few of the Boy's Day decorations.

If a family has the space and equipment, they may hoist koinobori (鯉のぼり), which are windsocks made to look like carp. From the ancient Chinese myth, carp are believed to swim upstream to a source, and those reaching riverheads turn into dragons. Hence, it is a symbol of future success.

Boy's Day treats are usually kashiwamochi (柏餅), rice cakes wrapped in oak leaves. As oak leaves do not fall until new shoots appear, they symbolise unbroken family lineage. Some regions make chimaki (ちまき), which is cooked rice wrapped in bamboo leaves. This is a tradition borrowed from a Chinese festival commemorating the death of poet Qu Yuan.

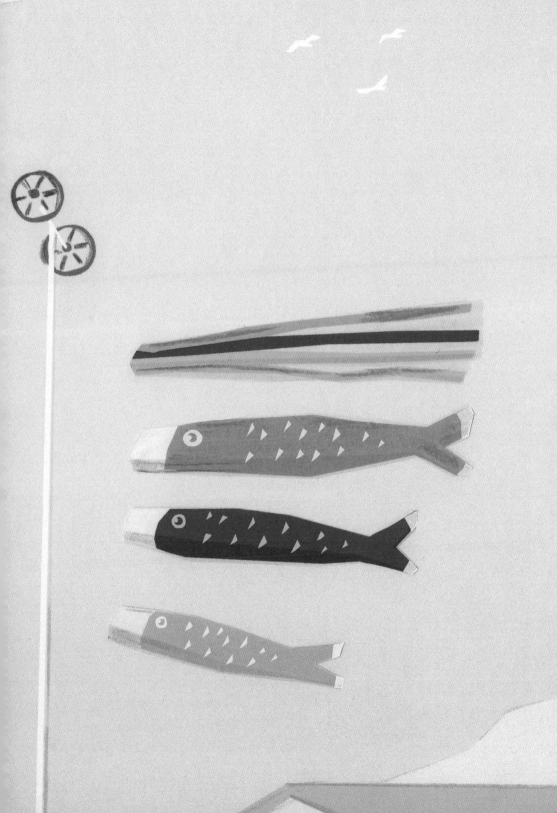

日 本 の 生 き 方

April: cherry blossom and back to school

Just as the English talk endlessly about the weather, the Japanese talk incessantly about the changing seasons. We do not miss a beat in reminding other people that we have four seasons in our country (but so did Vivaldi, for crying out loud). It is an important part of what we are, though, and nothing is more important, in the context of the seasonal transformations, than the blooming of the cherry blossom in spring.

Appreciating cherry blossom *en masse* for its beauty alone is a relatively recent phenomenon, dating back to the Edo period, when city dwellers had become the cultural force. Since then, the way we appreciate the blooming has not changed much – alcohol consumption during daytime and beyond.

The flowering of the cherry blossom coincides with the end and beginning of the Japanese academic year. When we adopted our Western-style public education system, bureaucrats didn't see why the academic year should differ from the government's fiscal year, from April to March of the following year (it was taken from the British).

There is some talk of aligning the Japanese academic year with the rest of the world to start in autumn and ending in summer. Apart from the ease of transferring between overseas and domestic education systems, a more serious argument is that it would be better not to leave kids unattended for a month and a half of summer holiday after only three months of the new school year, lest all that has been crammed into their tiny brains be drained in the heat of summer. While the arguments for change have some force, it is unlikely to happen. The Japanese are too attached to having the cherry blossom as a backdrop to the beginning of new chapters in their lives.

June: the rainy season

Japan's geographic location exposes it to East Asian monsoons. At the beginning of every summer, warm air over the Pacific Ocean pushes back relatively cold air above the Asian continent, creating a weather front that brings rain. The longer it takes for Team Pacific to push Team Asia away, the longer the rainy season continues.

While rain is not a pleasant weather phenomenon, especially when accompanied with the rising humidity and temperature of an oceanic climate, the Japanese have long appreciated the benefits that the seasonal rain brings. *Megumi no ame* (恵みの雨) is our term for the 'benevolence of rain'.

The fresh water supply of Japan's river systems relies on two sources and one key factor. One source is winter snowfall, and the other is seasonal rain. The key factor is the ability of mountains to soak it up and act as natural reservoirs. Due to our population explosion, Japan has built many reservoir dams in the mountains at considerable cost, both financial and environmental. Whether or not more are needed is a topic for heated political debate, both locally and nationally.

July: the summer holidays

As explained, the Japanese school year begins in April, while the summer holidays usually start in the middle of July. This means that teachers worry about children's learning if they're leaving so soon after the start of the new term for a month and half. Therefore, teachers, especially in primary schools, usually pile homework and assignments on children to be done during the holiday.

Although their lives may be hijacked by PlayStation and Xbox, a child's typical summer holiday would feature at least some of the following:

Swimming pools: Schools have pools, and open them to the public during the holidays. This prompts children to go back to school voluntarily, but just to exhaust themselves splashing about and to catch up with their friends.

A visit to the beach: As an island nation, Japan has no shortage of seaside, and no summer family outing is complete without at least one visit to the beach. Usually, the game of *suikawari* (スイカ割り) is played, in which a blindfolded player attempts to find and crack open a *suika*, or watermelon, by hitting it with a stick while the spectators try to navigate the player. Even if you know where the watermelon is, you are not supposed to hit it with too much force and crush it to smithereens – cool and juicy watermelon is one of summer's unmissable delights.

A visit to the mountains: There is relatively cool air during the summer in the peaks, especially compared to the concrete jungle below. The mountains are also heaven for children who have a fascination with insects. Apart from ever-annoying mosquitos, there are colourful butterflies to be observed and noisy cicadas to be caught. The king of them all is the beetle. Especially valued are *kabutomushi* (カブトムシ – rhinoceros beetles), with their unicorn-like horn, and *kuwagata mushi* (クワガタムシ – stag beetles), with antler-like pincer jaws. These beetles have become so popular that there are people running businesses of growing and selling them at a high price.

August: Obon

August is the height of summer in Japan. The sun beats down mercilessly, and the asphault roads feel like frying pans. People move slowly if forced to go outside. They tend to lock themselves up at home with air-con watching high-school baseball on TV.

It is also the month of *Obon* (お盆), the Japanese version of what is known in China as the 'Hungry Ghost Festival'. It comes from the Buddhist parable about the sorrow of one of Buddha's followers for his deceased parents, who are suffering in their afterlives as *gaki* (餓鬼), or eternally hungry ghosts. To ease his conscience, Buddha told the man that the ghosts would be permitted to return home for a limited period and that he could take care of them during that time to ease their suffering. The tradition came to Japan with the introduction of Buddhism, then mingled with its indigenous ancestral worship to become *Obon*. Celebrated on 15th August, *Obon* is a family affair, and people tend to return to their ancestral homes for this occasion.

In my family, my late grandmother made a big fuss of the festival. She cleaned the family *butsudan* (仏壇), or Buddhist altar, especially for the occasion, and decorated it with fresh flowers and special lanterns. Then she told us children to go to the temple where our family cemetery was, with a handheld lantern and unlit candles. At the cemetery, we were to summon the ancestral spirits and light a candle in the lantern, even in the bright daylight of the August sun. It was supposed to light the way back home for the spirits, she said. Arriving at home, grandmother did an amazing piece of play-acting, welcoming each of the ancestors she had known personally by addressing them each in turn. The spirits stayed at home for three nights and four days, sharing mealtimes with the living (a small set of dishes were served at the family altar). On the fourth day, we led the spirits to the bank of a riverside, or any waterway, and saw them off back to the afterlife by making a little bonfire. This was, of course, the climax of my grandmother's performance, saying her goodbyes to all the spirits, presumably floating downriver to the world of the dead.

A lighter form of entertainment during *Obon* period is *bonodori* (盆踊り), or an *Obon* dance party. Each local community builds a makeshift platform in a public space, and people dance around it after sundown to traditional Japanese music, usually clad in *yukata*, the type of *kimono* made with thin cotton cloth. As a child, my parents forbid me from attending *bonodori*, saying it was sleazy. It does have an atmosphere of permissiveness, with everyone wearing somewhat revealing *yukata*, and the thin cloth silhouetting the wearers' bodies. When the prohibition was declared, I was too small to care about girls. In later teenage years, my younger brother managed to sneak out of our house to take part in the party, and proved himself to be very popular with the opposite sex (or so the rumour went). That put me off *bonodori* forever, as there was no way I wanted to be upstaged by my little brother. Especially in front of girls.

September–November: autumn harvest festivals

The Japanese word for autumn is *aki* (秋). It is said that the word comes from *akiru*, which means 'getting tired of', because people wished for a harvest so abundant that they would get tired of too much food.

Once the crops are harvested, it is time to celebrate. Throughout Japan, there are festivals held in local shrines, with a focus on giving thanks to the gods for a good harvest, or, in the case of bad years, praying for a better harvest in the next year.

Shinto festivals usually feature the parading of *mikoshi* (神輿), or a portable altar. These are attached to two planks and are meant to be carried around on peoples' shoulders. The average *mikoshi* weighs about 500kg (there are some weighing over a ton). Shrines usually have their own societies of *mikoshi*-bearers who, at festival time, don the traditional attire of *happi* (法被), or *hanten* (半纏), both types of a short, jacket-style kimono, and walk about the neighbourhood with their *mikoshi* on their shoulders with much gusto.

Autumn is also the season when people start being active again after the unbearable summer heatwave. There are slogans such as 'Autumn is for Sports' or 'Autumn for Arts', encouraging people to engage in activities. By far the most popular slogan is 'Autumn is for Healthy Appetite', encouraging people to gorge on the fruits of the harvest.

Autumn is also for indulging in another typically Japanese activity of enjoying the changing seasons. In a custom called *momijigari* (紅葉狩り), or 'hunting for autumn colours', people go outdoors to appreciate the changing leaves on the trees. While it isn't as boisterous as the hunt for the spring cherry blossom, the mountains nevertheless are filled with people in search of visual treats. Famous spots like Karasawa in Nagano prefecture see large 'villages' of tent-dwellers springing up to take part in this outdoor visual feast.

December: the end of the year

In old Japanese, December was called *shiwasu* (師走) meaning that the masters (*shi*) were running about (*su*) being busy.

Today December is also a busy month. The business world tries to get as much done as possible before the year-end, as little is achieved with the New Year holiday mood in January, and then you are only the short month of February away from the end of the fiscal year in March. December is not a good month for business trips to Japan.

Towards the end of the month, we have the current emperor's birthday on the 23rd, which is a public holiday. Christmas Eve on the 24th is somehow regarded as romantic in Japan, like most of the newly imported Western customs are (like Valentine's Day). Young couples are expected to go on dates and cheeky restaurants hike their prices for the day.

The 30th is called *misoka* (晦日), or the 'last day of the month' – a custom dating back to the days of the lunar calendar, where each month usually consisted of 30 days. Offices usually close on or before the 30th, and each workplace holds what is called *shigoto osame* (仕事納め), or 'closing of work', perhaps with a little speech from the boss and exchanges of good wishes among the colleagues for the new year.

The 31st is known as Ōmisoka (大晦日), or the 'great last day of the month', because it is also the end of the year. People are back at home, busy with preparations to welcome in the coming year, cooking traditional New Year's dishes, and carrying out ōsōji (大掃除), or the 'grand cleaning', to get rid of the bad luck of the past year and to welcome in good luck for the new year.

Towards midnight, all the Buddhist temples throughout Japan start banging their gongs 108 times. The number 108 represents the number of cares that each person carries in his or her life in accordance with Buddhist teaching. With each toll of the gong, people are expected to let go of their cares and be ready for the New Year. People go to bed with the sound of gongs ringing out in the dark, cold night, to close the old year and welcome the new one come morning.

Brimming with creative inspiration, how-to projects and useful information to enrich your everyday life, Quarto Knows is a favourite destination for those pursuing their interests and passions. Visit our site and dig deeper with our books into your area of interest: Quarto Creates, Quarto Cooks, Quarto Homes, Quarto Lives, Quarto Drives, Quarto Explores, Quarto Gifts, or Quarto Kids.

First published in 2018 by White Lion Publishing,
an imprint of The Quarto Group.
The Old Brewery, 6 Blundell Street,
London, N7 9BH,
United Kingdom
T (0)20 7700 6700 F (0)20 7700 8066
www.QuartoKnows.com

Every effort has been made to trace the copyright holders of material quoted in this book. If application is made in writing to the publisher, any omissions will be included in future editions.

A catalogue record for this book is available from the British Library.

ISBN 978 1 78131 761 7
Ebook ISBN 978 1 78131 847 8

10 9 8 7 6 5 4 3 2 1

Design by Akihiro Nakayama
Illustrations by Taku Bannai
Photography by Shohki Eno

All photography courtesy of Shohki Eno with the following exceptions:
p.42 Japan: Empress Jit (645 - 703) at a palace door looking out at the wooded mountains of Kaguyama. Utagawa Kuniyoshi (1797-1861), c. 1841 / Pictures from History / Bridgeman Images
p.160 ©Studio Ghibli, courtesy of Everett Collection/Alamy
        ©Studio Ghibli, courtesy of Photo 12 / Alamy Stock Photo
p.164 Photo of 'Full House' ©Philip Arneill / www.tokyojazzjoints.com
p.187, 188 below ©Shutterstock
p.188 above ©Larisa Blinova / Alamy Stock Photo

Shohki would like thank the following people and locations for their help with the project:
p.6 Artist: Taichi Inoue, 井上太市
p.48-9 Location: Tenonji, 天恩山五百羅漢寺
p.153 Location: Igo salon TENGEN Shinjyuku, 囲碁サロン 天元 新宿
p.156 Location: Mugenryu Tokyo International Karatedo
p.162 Location: Studio circus